Dookie, Sookie, and Big Mo

by Alice Mertie Underhill

Cover and illustrations by James Converse

TEACH Services, Inc.
New York

2010 11 12 13 14 · 5 4 3 2 1

Copyright © 2003, 2006 TEACH Services, Inc.
ISBN-13: 978-1-57258-255-2
Library of Congress Control Number: 2003102655

Published by

TEACH Services, Inc.
www.TEACHServices.com

Contents

The village charm doctor, carrying a torch and a string of bones and shells, stepped forward and began the usual dance and chanting song.

Big Mo Was Too Late

THERE was excitement in the Savara village in India. On this morning people were hurrying to and from the market; but there was an unusual restlessness, for something was about to happen. Mothers held their babies in their arms, and took the small hands of their young children as they hastened along the street to the road that led down to the river. Dogs barked and ducks quacked, and chickens squawked as they flew across the road to get out of the way.

"Big Mo, where is everybody going?" asked Kola, the herdboy, as he drove a small herd of cows from the river road toward the grasslands near the bank of the river.

"There's going to be a funeral, Kola," answered Big Mo. "I didn't know about it until I came to sell the milk, or I would have told you when you came to get the cows. Everything should be ready by now." Then, taking long strides, the big man of the village soon joined the crowd that was making its way to the clearing.

"I'm going, too," said Kola to himself. He put down the big stick he was carrying. He would leave the cows to graze in the tall green grass. He was certain they would not stray far with plenty of grass to eat. The funeral would not take long, if, as Big Mo said, they had everything ready. Kola hurried to overtake the big man of the village.

When he came to the clearing, Kola saw a great pile of logs, dry grass, and twigs. Partly covered in this was a body wrapped in a dark cloth. On the top of the body was a small bundle, the object of much conversation among the people standing about.

"Is that little bundle the baby?" asked Kola, as he stood beside Big Mo.

"Yes, Kola, the mother died in childbirth."

"But why burn the baby, too, when it is still alive?" Kola asked anxiously.

"Sh—Kola," said Big Mo. "It has long been the custom of the Savaras to do it this way. Our people feel that it is more merciful, for without the mother's milk the child will slowly starve to death anyway. This way is quick—no long-drawn-out agony."

2

"But to burn the baby alive." Kola shuddered as he spoke. His eyes were wide with awe and wonder. He had been to funerals before, of course, for births and deaths are common events in India; but somehow this one was different.

Kola and Big Mo stood in silence in the crowd. The village charm doctor, dressed in his ceremonial costume, with decorated headdress, strings of bones and shells, and an embroidered sash and beaded sandals, stepped forward. He was carrying a burning torch in his hand. He began with the usual weird dance and chanting song, which were supposed to drive away the evil spirits, and then he signaled to his helper, who stepped up to the dry grass and twigs and started a fire.

Big Mo clenched his fists as he heard the sound of wailing from the relatives and friends. Even some of the curious onlookers screamed and shed tears as the flames leaped up and enveloped the funeral pyre on which the dead mother and her living newborn infant were lying.

Kola trembled. He feared the anger of the spirits. He shared the great superstition of the people in the village.

"The baby! The baby!" someone cried. "Don't let the baby burn!"

Then a fearful silence fell on the crowd as the charm doctor called down the spirits to quiet the people. Big Mo turned his face away. Had he only imagined it, or had he heard the tiny baby cry out in the flames? He could not be sure.

Something inside him stirred; his heart beat rapidly. If only he dared to snatch it from the burning pyre before it was too late!

But, no, there stood the charm doctor calling the wrath of the spirits upon the villagers. There stood the relatives and friends weeping silently. Big Mo was powerless to help. The crowd began moaning and screaming again. Mothers clutched their own little ones and turned to leave. It was too awful to see, and yet the whole village had come to witness it.

Big Mo waited until most of the people had gone. When he was certain that the charm doctor was out of sight, he went over to the burning mass. Kola held back, wondering what his friend was going to do. There was no sound but the crackling of the flames. With his bare hands the man reached into the fire and pulled out the small bundle; but it crumbled as it fell at his feet. He was too late! But that was how it was when the spirits were angry—only trouble, curses, and death.

"How did you dare?" asked Kola, looking at Big Mo's burned hands. "Do you have no fear of the spirits? They will put a terrible curse on you."

"I did not think of what the spirits might do to me," said Mo. "I could think only of that helpless baby. I thought I heard it cry. I am almost sure I heard it."

As Big Mo and Kola followed the stragglers

along the river road, Kola asked, "But how could you hear it with the noise of the fire, the people screaming, and the charm doctor shouting and chanting?"

"Maybe I just felt it in here," said Big Mo, touching his chest. "Here in my heart something tells me it is not right to burn babies this way. But what can we do? We are powerless to stop it. Anyway, I tried to save it, but I was too late."

"Big Mo," began Kola, "I know you are the strong man of our village, and I like to work for you. But when you dare to say things against the charm doctor and the spirits, you make me afraid." Kola ran ahead, picked up his stick, and went over to where the cows were grazing contentedly on the green grass.

"Well," mused Big Mo to himself, as he walked back to the village, "I thought Kola was my friend, but perhaps he isn't."

Big Mo sold his milk and made a few purchases in the market. Then he went to the spring, washed out his big milk jars, and filled them with cool water from the spring. He started home, but he paused for a moment before the shrine under the spirit tree. On the stones before the shrine he placed a bouquet of flowers that he had purchased at the market. After he had chanted the weird song of the charm doctor, he climbed the stony hill path to his mud hut. He set the jars full of water on the hard dirt floor, took a bottle of oil from the shelf, and rubbed

5

some on his blistered hands. There was an ache in his heart as he thought of the tiny infant he had been powerless to save.

"If only I had dared to go sooner, I could have saved it," he muttered under his breath. (The spirits might be angry if he spoke his thoughts aloud.) "Someday I will do something about it!" Then Big Mo went to work in his paddy terrace.

All through the hot day his imagination brought back a tiny baby's cry. Over and over he said to himself, "I was too late, too late!"

When the sun was low in the western sky, Mo went home. Soon he heard the click, click of cows' hoofs on the sharp stones of the hill path. Mo opened the gate of the little enclosure behind the house, and Kola drove the cows in.

"Kola," began Mo, as he closed the gate, "I have been thinking about what we saw this morning."

"So have I," said Kola; "but I'm afraid to talk about it. The spirits may hear and put a terrible curse on me. I must hurry." Waving good-by with his goading stick, the youth ran down the path and was soon lost from sight.

Big Mo turned to his evening chores. He milked the cows, strained the milk into a clean earthen jar, and set it in the water tank to cool. He ate his supper of beans and rice, built a small fire for protection outside the door of the hut, and sat down on the stone step.

There was a heavy ache in his heart as he

watched the moon come up behind the palm trees beyond the lotus pool. It was a beautiful moon. There must be a powerful spirit who could make the moon rise in the sky. Could it be the same spirit that made the sun come up in the morning? There must also be spirits that made the rain for the paddy fields, that made the rice grow, that kept water in the spring and in the river. Surely these were good spirits. They would not put tiny babies on the funeral pyre to be burned alive!

"Someday I will find out about all this," said Big Mo, clenching his fists. "Someday I will know if the good spirits are stronger than the evil spirits." Mo closed the bamboo gate in front of the door of the hut to keep out prowlers. Then he stretched out on his mat on the dirt floor inside and went to sleep.

Big Mo lifted his opponent Thau up in his strong arms, held him up
above his head, then threw him down on the dusty ground with a thud.

The Challenger

THE next morning the sun rose over the palm trees beyond the river. Mo milked the cows, ate his breakfast, and prepared to go to the village to sell the milk. He could hear Kola singing as he came up the path. The song, in a weird minor key, echoed from the jungle. It was the chant of the charm doctor, the song that was supposed to keep away the evil spirits. As Kola passed the shrine under the spirit tree, he wanted to make sure that only good spirits followed him.

Brief were the greetings between Kola and Mo as the man opened the gate to let the cows out. Waving his goad stick with a flourish, the boy drove the cows down the path.

"He must be angry with me," said Big Mo to

himself, "because of what happened yesterday. Perhaps he will forget about it and talk to me again. I'll wait and see."

As Mo worked in the hut he heard singing outside the door. Thinking Kola had returned, Mo said, "Come in, Kola."

When the man turned his head, he saw in the doorway the wizened form of the charm doctor!

"Good news I bring you," began the charm doctor in his cracked, high-pitched voice, as he stepped lightly into the hut. "Good news for both of us."

"What is the good news?" inquired Mo.

"It is Big Thau," said the little man, shaking the strings of bones and shells that hung around his neck. "Big Thau is in the village this morning, and he wants to challenge you to a fight. There's money in it for you if you accept." He patted the money bag that he carried inside the folds of his garment. Then he added, "We know who will win."

Big Mo had heard of the fame of Big Thau from the neighboring village, and he had often wished he could meet him in a fight. But today, with his hands still sore from the flames, he would not have a chance.

"How can I fight with these?" he asked, extending his hands.

"I can fix it," said the charm doctor in his high-pitched voice.

"But I fight square and honest. I don't want

10

any tricks when I meet a challenger. I am big and strong, and I can hold my own with anyone. But just now it would be unfair. Tell Big Thau to wait a few days; then I will accept."

The charm doctor looked again at Mo's hands. Then he pointed up to the big gourd hanging by a fiber cord from a peg in the corner of the room.

"Tsu—that will do it!" he beamed. His eyes gleamed in anticipation of a good drink from it himself.

Mo knew that the tsu, rice whisky, would soon deaden the charm doctor's sensibilities. Without further argument Mo took down the gourd, poured a drink for his guest, and then, taking his milk jars and the liquor gourd, followed the charm doctor out the door.

Big Mo took big strides as he went down the path to the village road. The charm doctor had to run to keep up with him. When they came to the village they noticed a crowd had gathered on the wide street in front of the market. People were watching Big Thau exhibit his strength by lifting heavy weights. Children were thrilled as he permitted them to feel the huge muscles in his arms.

Suddenly the crowd parted and people shouted, "Here comes Big Mo! I bet he is stronger than Big Thau!"

Everyone stood back as the two giants met on the village street. When Big Mo had put down the milk jars and the big gourd, he walked fearlessly up to the challenger. Without hesitation they began their exhibition of strength, as each one wrestled and tried to throw the other. Soon the wrestling changed to hitting, and the excited crowd shouted, "Come on, Big Mo, hit him again! You can get him down!"

The charm doctor stood back in the crowd. Now he was not so positive of the outcome of the fight. Big Mo was holding his own in spite of his burned hands. "Tsu in the big gourd!" shouted the little man. The fighters paused for a few moments, took long drinks of liquor from the gourd, and then with fiery gleams in their eyes they went at it again. Part of the crowd was cheering Thau, while others were shouting words of encouragement to Big Mo. Children jumped up and down, calling, "Come on, Big Mo, you can do it!"

Big Mo lifted Thau up in his strong arms, held him up above his head, and then threw him down on the dusty ground with a thud! Big Mo towered over him, breathing rapidly. His eyes gleamed, his bruised and bleeding lips showed a big smile of triumph. He had won again, in spite of the sore and burning hands. He lightly touched the prone body of Thau with his bare foot.

"Someday I will get you for this," said the defeated man. "It may take a long time, but I will get you, someday."

Mo wiped his sweaty face and chest with a

piece of cloth, and looked for the charm doctor. Since he was not in sight, Mo decided to visit him later and collect the money.

Men went back to work, while the women took their children and went to the market to finish shopping. The man on the ground arose slowly, rubbed his injured arm and leg, and limped down the road toward the market. As Big Mo watched his opponent go, he picked up his gourd and milk jugs. After selling the milk, he went up the hill path toward home.

Arriving at his hut, Big Mo wiped the perspiration from his face, and put oil on his bleeding lips and sore arms and hands. He decided not to go out to the rice fields in the hot sun. The work could wait until another day. The man spread a blanket on the floor and stretched out. It would be a long time before Kola would bring the cows home. Big Mo was tired; it had been a hard fight. But he had won in spite of his sore, blistered hands. He was still the village champion. Someday, perhaps, he would be the best fighter in India! Perhaps not in all India, but in the land of the Savaras, anyway. He clenched his fists and tightened his muscles. How big and strong he felt! How good it made him feel to hear the people cheer!

He recalled the day at the raja's garden party, when he had been asked to show his strength to some of the raja's rich and honored friends. How proud he felt when he held back the car from

13

moving, with the motor going at full power. The raja paid him well for that performance!

Big Mo wiped the blood from his lips again, as he closed his eyes. In a few minutes he was asleep with a satisfied smile on his face.

The sun was nearing the western horizon when Big Mo suddenly awoke. He sat up quickly, for he heard singing. It was Kola coming up the stony path, bringing the four cows home. Mo arose and went to open the gate.

"I heard about the fight," said Kola. "People in the village say you are the strongest man for miles around—you can whip anybody."

Big Mo felt pride coursing through him. He liked to have people say how strong he was. He was glad that Kola was in a mood to talk. Perhaps they could be friends after all. Mo shut the gate after Kola drove the cows into the enclosure.

"Did you have a good day in the grasslands?" Kola nodded.

"It must have been hot in the valley," said Mo. Kola nodded again.

"Will you stay and eat supper with me, Kola?"

"No," said Kola. "You are a strong man; but you dare to go against the spirits. I would be afraid to eat with you. Besides, you have been drinking too much from the big gourd." With a wave of his goad, Kola went on his way, singing the chant of the charm doctor.

Big Mo turned to the task of preparing rice in the black kettle that hung in the little fireplace. When it was cooking, he took the milk bucket and went to milk the cows. Big Mo strained the milk through a white cloth into an earthen jar. Then he placed the jar in the water tank to cool. He did not need to add water to the milk he sold, as many people did, for Mo was a "four-cow" man, and considered quite rich. Most of his neighbors owned only one cow.

Before he retired for the night, Big Mo, as usual, built a fire near the door for protection against wild jungle animals. Tigers, leopards, wild jungle dogs, hyenas, and monkeys often came down from the hills to snatch whatever they could find. Big Mo knew that wild animals are afraid of fire, so he felt safer as the flames threw their light on his mat on the floor.

Mo sat down on his stone doorstep to watch the moon come up over the palm trees. As he sat thinking, he gently rubbed oil on his hands and his bruised lips. He was not sleepy, for he had spent the afternoon in drunken drowsiness. Perhaps Kola was right in saying that he drank too much.

Spindlelegs

S BIG MO sat on the stone step, he heard the frequent bawling of one of the cows in the enclosure. "I'd better see that all is well with my herd," he said to himself. When he reached the enclosure, he saw a new-born calf lying on the ground near the fence corner. The mother cow was standing over it, uttering low moos of reassurance as she licked it with her tongue.

"What have we here?" said Mo, gently patting the cow. "Now I am a rich man, indeed, with five cows. I will take a generous gift to the charm doctor in the morning. The spirits have blessed me again."

With his big hands Big Mo helped the wobbly calf to her feet, but she was so unsteady that he put her down again.

16

"Shall we try it again?" asked Big Mo a little later, as he lifted the calf to her feet and put her soft, warm nose close to the cow.

"There you are," he said softly. "You will need some milk to give you strength to grow. Careful, little girl, you are not very steady on those spindlelegs. Easy now; not too fast at first. That's right, Spindlelegs, you can do it!"

With the help of Mo's strong hands the calf soon found nourishment, but after a few minutes of feeding, she lay down again to rest.

"Take a long rest now, Spindlelegs," he said. When Big Mo returned to the doorstep, he was tempted to take another drink from the big gourd; but he remembered Kola's words.

"I wonder if the moon is lonely," mused Big Mo, as he looked at its silvery disk. "Like me, it does not have a companion. The mother cow has Spindlelegs, the birds and animals of the jungle have their mates; but here I am, all alone, no one to talk to, no one to share my home. Even my friend, Kola, avoids me. The charm doctor comes up the hill to see me now and then, but only to receive gifts for the spirits, to make arrangements for fights, or to drink from the gourd."

The spirits must have been pleased with Big Mo, for no great misfortune had ever come to him. But he could not talk to the spirits.

"Why? Why?" he kept saying to himself. Then suddenly he arose, placed a few sticks of wood on the fire, and went into the hut. "I still have one friend," he said. He went to the corner of the room, lifted the gourd from the peg, and took a long drink. He wiped his mouth; the liquor stung his sore lips. Then he replaced the gourd on the peg.

A Cry in the Night

SUDDENLY Big Mo heard a strange sound. Perhaps it was the cry of an animal, for there were many strange sounds in the jungle at night. Then it came again—a pitiful sound like a child crying. Yet this was common, for the leopards and panthers made a sound like that.

"Maybe I have been drinking too freely from the big gourd," said Big Mo. "I am hearing strange noises. Next I will be seeing strange things. Kola was right; I have been drinking too much for my good."

He heard it again. Was it an animal growling? The sound seemed to be coming from the direction of the path that led to the house. Big Mo took one of the burning sticks from the fire, held it high as a torch, and peered into the darkness.

19

He caught a glimpse of three wild dogs of the jungle snarling and snapping at each other. They seemed to be quarreling over something on the ground. One of the dogs was walking backward up the hill, dragging something, shaking it now and then in his teeth. As Big Mo came closer, the dogs growled savagely. Holding the torch closer, Mo could see that there was something moving, something alive, in the bundle.

"Go away!" shouted Mo, waving the flaming stick at the dogs. They snapped fiercely, but then backed away, slipping quietly into the darkness of the jungle.

Mo held the torch so that he could see what the dogs had been dragging. From inside the depths of the dirty cloth wrapping there came a pitiful cry. It was not the cry of an animal; it was the cry of a human baby! Mo pushed aside the corner of the blanket. It was a baby—a tiny brown baby.

Gently Mo lifted the bundle and carried it to the house. He looked back to see if the dogs were following him, but they were nowhere to be seen. As he felt the squirming, crying infant struggle in the blanket, his heart gave a leap. This one was alive! This bundle did not crumble in his hands as had the one on the funeral pile. Suppose this was a baby that had been on a funeral pile! But how did the dogs get it? Dogs are afraid of fire. How could they snatch it from the flames?

"Go away!" shouted Mo, waving the flaming stick at the dogs. They snapped fiercely, then backed away, slipping quietly into the jungle.

Mo carried the bundle to the house, put another stick on the fire, and sat down to examine the contents of the bundle.

"What have we here?" he said as he held the little one on his lap. The baby was fastened in a dirty blanket, covered with leaves and stickers. One corner of the blanket had been torn by the sharp teeth of the dogs. As Mo examined the blanket he saw that this was not the usual wrapping for babies about to be burned; this was not a dark little shroud, but a light wrapping blanket, the kind mothers used on the tiny ones to protect their tender skin from the hot sun.

As the baby cried piteously, Big Mo removed the blanket. He noticed that the infant's back was scratched and bleeding from being dragged over the sharp stones on the path.

"This will never do," he said, arising and going into the house. He lighted the lamp on the bench, poured water into the basin, and gently bathed the tiny back. The baby cried, even though Big Mo was as gentle as he could be with his rough hands.

"Don't cry, tiny one," he said soothingly. "I am trying not to hurt you."

After the cooling bath, Mo patted on some oil, and the crying ceased for a few moments.

"You feel better now, don't you?" said Mo. "Now to find something to wrap you in; your blanket is too dirty." An idea came to him. "Strainers!" he said. "I have plenty of new white milk strainers. They are soft and white and clean. I will wrap you in a milk strainer!"

When Big Mo had wrapped the baby in a clean white milk strainer, he sat down to look at her. She was so small and helpless. She puckered up her mouth and began to cry.

"Now don't do that again," said Mo. Then he realized that she was probably hungry. Little Spindlelegs, too, was small and helpless, but she could get up on her wobbly legs and find dinner to give her strength. But this baby had no mother. How long had she been without food? When Big Mo lifted her to his cheek, the baby felt around with its mouth for something to eat.

"I guess it is up to me to do something," said Mo. "But what do babies eat when there isn't a mother? Rice? No, without teeth she couldn't eat rice."

In some cases Mo had heard that people had used rice water mixed with rice whisky. "Not the drink from the big gourd," said Mo, shaking his head. "That would never do. It would be much too strong for this little one. It is even too strong for me."

Suddenly one of the cows bawled out in the enclosure, and again Mo thought of Spindlelegs. People in the village did not feed their babies cow's milk; that was for the calves. Surely there must be something! The baby might starve to death right here in his arms. Just then Spindlelegs called, "Maaaa."

23

"All right, Spindlelegs, if it is good enough for you, it should be good enough for the tiny one—for tonight, anyway. I can't let her starve. I will mix up something."

The milk in the big jug was still warm. Mo placed the baby on his sleeping mat while he dipped milk into a coconut shell. Then he poured in a little water and sweetened it with a few drops of honey.

"Perhaps this will do for tonight," said Mo. "Tomorrow I will ask someone for advice."

Big Mo tore off a small piece of a new white strainer, dipped a corner into the mixture, and then squeezed the drops into the baby's open mouth. She swallowed the drops and cried again. Time after time Big Mo squeezed milk into the little mouth, and finally the baby was satisfied and went to sleep. As Big Mo held her in his arms, he wondered where she had come from. What would he do with her? What would the charm doctor do if he found a baby in Mo's house? What would Kola think? He would surely accuse him of taking one of those bundles from a funeral pyre. What would the village authorities do about it? He could not keep her hidden. Someone would be sure to tell. Big Mo decided he would carry her to the village in the morning when he took the milk to the market. He would tell his story and make inquiries. Surely she belonged to someone.

The baby stirred. Mo squeezed some more

24

milk into her mouth, and she slept again. Mo laid her down on his mat. Then he washed the soiled blanket in the basin and hung it on a bush to dry. He returned to the house, put the bamboo gate in front of the door, and stretched out on the mat beside the sleeping baby.

A Gift From the Spirits

FOR a long time Big Mo lay awake thinking. Surely the spirits were pleased with him. Had he not put flowers on the spirit tree shrine because of his burned hands, and had they not given the victory over Big Thau? Then there was Spindlelegs, the new calf. Now could it be that the spirits had brought this baby to him because he was lonely? If he took her to the village authorities, would the spirits be angry? Would they put a curse upon him if he did not accept their gift?

"Oh, if I could only keep her," said Big Mo in a whisper, "I would be so happy. I would not be lonely."

The baby beside him stirred. He patted her gently with his big hand. He held his face close

26

and said comforting words. The baby stretched up her tiny hand and touched his cheek. It was a warm hand, reaching out to him for love and protection from the unfriendly world into which she had been born. Big Mo felt emotions he had never known before. He had saved the baby from a terrible death, and now she depended on him. She was utterly helpless; she needed him.

The tiny hand pressed lightly against his cheek was a pledge. He would keep her, care for her as a father. He would teach her many things; but above all, he would love her, and give her all the affection that he could. She was his gift from the spirits, and he would try to be worthy of that gift.

"I will keep her always," Mo decided. "I will give her a name; but I must take care. If I give her a good name, the spirits will think she is so nice they will take her from me. If I call her Dookie, which means grief, the spirits will not desire her. Poor little baby! She has had her share of grief in her short life. I will also give her my name, for she is a gift to me from the spirits. Dookie Mo; that will be her name."

When the baby awoke and cried, Big Mo fed her more diluted milk and honey. Then he turned her on her side so she would not be lying on her tender, scratched back. This time she slept soundly and for such a long time that Big Mo was worried. He put his ear close to her to make sure she was breathing. Then he extinguished the light, lay down, and soon was sleeping soundly.

The bright sun rose over the palm trees along the border of the river and shone in the open door of the hut, where Big Mo and Dookie, the tiny baby, lay sleeping.

The man awoke, stretched himself, sat up, and looked at the sleeping infant. He listened, but he could not hear her breathing! He touched her gently to see if she were still alive; she stirred lightly. With a sigh, Big Mo arose quietly, bathed his face in cool water, adjusted his garment, and prepared his breakfast. He put water and rice into the black kettle, placed it on the stones of the fireplace, and built a fire. Then he went to milk the cows. Soon Kola would be coming to take them to the valley where the green grass grew.

Spindlelegs was eating her breakfast. She was standing quite steadily, wagging her short tail vigorously. "You are doing all right, Spindlelegs," said Mo, patting her gently. "I knew you would make it if you kept trying."

When Big Mo finished milking, he strained the milk into the big jar, ready to take to the village. He kept a gourdful for the baby. She would soon wake up and be hungry. How tiny she looked, lying there on the sleeping mat, so helpless and dependent. She was a precious gift from the spirits.

Soon Big Mo heard the weird song which Kola sang as he came up the path. Big Mo wondered what Kola would say if he saw the baby. He would be sure to ask questions. Perhaps he would tell the police! The man hoped that the baby would sleep until Kola had gone with the cows. But just as Kola was passing the door of the house, Dookie began crying. Kola paused with his goad stick in his hand and peeked in the hut. There on Big Mo's sleeping mat was the baby.

When Big Mo told what had happened, Kola said, "You lie! You stole it from a funeral pyre, just as you tried to do that day when I was with you. Don't you fear the spirits or the curses of the charm doctor? How did you dare to steal it from the spirits?"

"But I didn't steal it!" insisted Big Mo, standing up tall and looking down into Kola's frightened face. "Have I ever lied to you, Kola?"

Kola shook his head.

Mo continued, "Would I lie about anything as tiny and helpless as that baby? Would I steal from the spirits who have been good to me? They gave me victory over the challenger, and brought me Spindlelegs, the new calf. If I stole the baby, I stole it from three savage dogs, who would have devoured it. How much better it is that she is alive, here in my home, where she is safe! I tell you, Kola, it was the spirits that brought her to me. The dogs were dragging her up the hill path. Look, her little back is scratched!"

29

Kola looked, and he was almost persuaded that Big Mo was telling him the truth. He had never known him to lie.

"I will keep her," said Big Mo. "I will protect her from harm. I will feed her, educate her, and give her a home as long as she will stay with me. I will love her, Kola, with all the love that I can give her. She needs me; she depends on me; she is so helpless!"

Kola stood as though stunned, looking at the baby. Slowly he shook his head. "I still can't make myself believe it," he said. Then suddenly he turned, dashed out the door, and ran to the enclosure for the cows. Waving his goad stick wildly, he chased the cows down the hill path so fast that he had to run to keep up with them.

Big Mo prepared some warm milk as before. Taking Dookie on his lap, he fed her as he had done the previous night. It took patience to feed the infant, but he was glad to do it. He must be very careful not to feed her too fast, or she might choke.

After Dookie had eaten all she wanted, Big Mo bathed the scratches on her back and put on more oil. He placed the baby on her tummy on the mat and covered her lightly with a cloth to keep off flies and insects. He set the coconut shell of milk in a bowl of water to keep out the ants.

Then Big Mo faced his problem: How was he going to carry two jars of milk and also carry the baby? He didn't dare to leave her alone until he returned. But how did men carry babies? Mothers carried them on their backs or in the folds of their saris while they worked. But men's garments were different—long, narrow strips of woven material wrapped several times around the body, with the red-fringed ends hanging down in back and front. Big Mo was puzzled. Finally he decided to hang the two jars from the ends of a long pole and balance them on his shoulder. Then he would loosen the folds of his garment and tuck the baby, wrapped in a strainer cloth, inside, safe from harm. With the jars balanced on the pole carried on his shoulder, he would be free to use his hands to care for Dookie.

Big Mo soon set out for the village, taking big strides as he went.

As Mo had anticipated, the villagers asked many questions. "Whose baby is it? Where did you get it? How are you going to fight with a baby on your hip?" People gathered around to see the big man with a tiny baby. Some laughed, but Mo did not care. Some gave him advice about caring for her. He was glad for their interest and friendliness. He made a few inquiries, but nobody seemed to know anything about the infant. The only funeral had been that of a man who had died of a fever. There was no baby involved in this case. Even the charm doctor seemed uninformed.

"Don't you think I would be the first to

know?" queried the charm doctor in his high-pitched voice, as he shook the string of bones and shells that hung around his neck. "The spirits do strange things; but I have ways of finding out. There was no 'mother funeral' since you burned your hands."

Big Mo went to the authorities of the village and told his story. They listened with interest, and the headman said, "You are a good man, Mo. I see no reason why you should not keep her. You are the reason she is still alive. Take her home and be gentle with her. Remember, you are a big man and she is very small. Better cut down a little with your drinking, too. You might neglect her at such times, you know."

"Yes," said Big Mo meekly. "Kola has told me I drink too much from the gourd. I will cut down, for her sake." And he pointed to the baby.

"What are you going to call her?" asked the headman.

"Dookie, which means grief. I will keep her, protect her, and care for her as my own daughter. I can raise her properly, for I am not a poor man. She is a precious gift from the spirits, and I dare anyone to try to take her from me, now that you say it is right for me to keep her." With these words Big Mo turned and went his way.

The Missing Baby

THE next morning Big Mo awoke and slipped quietly from his mat in order not to awaken little Dookie. He bathed his face and rubbed oil on his hands, which were healing fast. He saw that the bamboo gate in front of the door was up to keep out prowling animals, and then hurried to the cattle enclosure. If Dookie should awaken and cry, he would hear her. Kola would soon come to take the cows to graze. Again, the mother cow and Spindlelegs would remain in the enclosure. He would give the mother some jungle grass and water.

"Well, Spindlelegs, you will soon be strong enough to go down to the grasslands with your mother. Someday you will be a cow."

When Big Mo finished milking, he went to the

33

house, set the jar on the hard earth floor, and reached for a strainer. Suddenly his heart seemed to stand still. He looked at the mat, but the baby was not there!

He looked around the room. Something must have taken her. Since he had put up the bamboo gate, it must be a person. A big lump rose in his throat. Who could have taken his baby? Not Kola; he would be afraid of the spirits. The charm doctor? Big Mo clenched his fists. "If he has taken her from me, or harmed her in any way, spirits or no spirits, I will break every bone in his body!"

Big Mo went outside to look. Far down the hill path he saw someone carrying something. Without hesitation Big Mo started forward, taking big strides. Whoever it was became frightened and quickly disappeared in the jungle brush. Mo followed, pushed aside the tangled bushes, and found a small woman crouching there with Dookie clutched tightly in her arms.

"Who are you? Why did you take my baby?" he cried, dragging the woman out to the path. He took the tiny bundle from her, saying, "What right have you to take her? She is mine, I tell you, mine!"

Meekly the woman stood looking up into the angry face of the big man. "I know you must be very angry with me," she said. "But will you let me tell you my story?"

"Yes," said Big Mo, with a bit of kindness in

"Who are you? Why did you take my baby?" he cried, dragging the woman out to the path. "What right have you to take her?" he asked angrily.

his voice. The woman looked sad, timid, and frightened. Surely she had a reason for taking the baby. He would be a gentleman and listen.

"I am Resa," she began, her head bowed. "She is my baby, and I was taking her back to the spirit shrine, for it will only bring more trouble to her and to me, and perhaps to you."

"But I swear I did not take her from the shrine," said Big Mo. "I do not know where she came from; but I found her right here on this path. She was being dragged across these sharp rocks by hungry jungle dogs. Look at her little back, all scratched and bruised. Now will you believe me? I could not leave her to be destroyed by them! I took her, bathed her sores, and put oil on her scratches. I fed her as best I knew. Surely the spirits were pleased that I did so. But you, the mother, left her alone on the shrine for wild animals to devour. Why did you do it?"

"The charm doctor told me it was the only thing I could do. You see—" She lowered her voice. "Because she is a girl the spirits were angry, and my husband died of the fever." The mother began to cry.

This was a new experience for Big Mo. He looked at the sobbing woman and he did not know what to do or say. It was only natural for her to cry, he reasoned; but he felt so awkward and helpless in her presence. He knew, of course, the superstitions of the Savaras. They believed that when a baby girl is born, the spirits are angry, and a great misfortune comes to the family. Usually, upon advice from the charm doctor, the spell is broken, and the spirits are satisfied if the baby girl is placed on the shrine under the spirit tree.

"But now," began Big Mo, "you have done your part. You have carried out the instructions of the charm doctor. Why will you anger the spirits more by taking her away from me? She is safe with me. You would only take her back where the dogs would find her and devour her. How could you, her mother, leave her there on the shrine, not knowing what would become of her? I heard her pitiful cry in the night. I heard the growling and snarling of the dogs as they fought over her. I saw the savage look in their eyes as I drove them away with a fire stick. I believe that the spirits gave her to me, and I intend to keep her."

Big Mo held the baby in his strong arms while the mother cried softly. The heart of the big man of the village was softened, and he asked with tenderness in his tone, "Tell me, Resa, now that you have done your part, why don't you keep your baby?"

Her eyes were filled with horror as she cried, "No, no! I would be afraid. The charm doctor said I must put her on the shrine or he would take her away. I am poor and with my husband dead, I must go to the city to find work. I cannot take the baby with me. I could not care for her."

Suddenly a thought came to her. She looked into Big Mo's eyes with trust and confidence. "Please, will you keep her? I will go away. I promise I will never see her again. I will put a few flowers on the shrine instead. Will you take care of her and be kind to her?"

"Yes," said Mo simply. "I will care for her as if she were my own daughter."

"Please." Resa held out her arms. "Please let me hold her once more; then I will go."

Thinking this might be a trick to take the baby from him, Big Mo hesitated. Then he realized that she knew her weakness. She could not run away from him. So he placed the bundle in her arms and the mother held her child for a brief moment. Then she put the baby back into the man's arms and ran down the path.

"Wait, Resa, come back!" called Big Mo; but the woman did not even hesitate. On she ran until she was out of sight beyond the big rocks.

Tenderly Mo carried Dookie back to the house. He held her lovingly against his bosom. Now she was really his, for the mother had given her to him to raise. Surely the spirits were satisfied. How carefully he would guard her! He would never leave her alone in the house again. There might be other dangers: wild animals or snakes or scorpions! He would guard her every moment. She was a special gift to him. He would take a present to the charm doctor this morning when he carried the milk to the village.

Big Mo put Dookie on the mat, strained the milk into the jars, and then prepared some warm milk in a coconut shell.

By this time little Dookie was crying for her breakfast. "Here you are, my precious one," said Big Mo, taking her in his arms and feeding her. "Slowly now, just a few drops at a time. I know you are hungry."

Before he had finished feeding Dookie, Kola came for the cows.

"Kola," called Big Mo from his seat on the floor, "will you throw some jungle grass to the mother cow? Then come into the house and I will give you your wages."

By the time Kola was ready to leave with the cows, Dookie had finished her breakfast. Big Mo placed her on the mat, took down his money box, and counted out the amount he owed Kola. He also added some extra coins as he placed them in Kola's hand.

"Rupees and annas!" exclaimed Kola with a big smile. "This is more than my wages."

"Because of the baby," said Big Mo. Then he added, "Your wages will be more next week, too, because you will be taking the mother cow and little Spindlelegs to the grasslands."

"Thank you," said Kola. "You are my good friend." He tucked the money into the folds of his garment, waved his goad stick in the air, and hurried to overtake the cows. Big Mo watched him go. Then he went to the corner of the room,

39

lifted the big gourd from the peg, and took a little drink. It had been some time since he had tasted rice liquor, and it seemed to stimulate his whole body with a glowing satisfaction. He was so happy! He would celebrate! The baby was his to keep! The headman of the village had said so—if he would cut down on his drinking. He replaced the gourd on the peg. One small drink would be enough.

The Big Thunder

DAY by day, as the baby grew stronger, Big Mo looked at her with wonder. "Dookie," he said, "you are growing. Someday you will be a big girl, and run about on those two brown feet. Someday you will talk to me in real words. You will grow up and be a woman, and then you will leave me. Sometimes I almost wish you would stay little like this, but I will always love you, my treasured gift from the spirits."

One hot, sultry day, when the ground was dry and hard around the thirsty rice plants and even the weeds seemed to wither in the hot sun, Big Mo walked from one end of the field to the other.

"We will go home early today, little Dookie," he said to the baby. "First we will go to the pond where the water is cool. There we will see the water buffaloes with their long, sweeping horns. They are fierce-looking animals, but they will not hurt you. Even the small boys scrub the animals' backs with coconut fiber while they lie in the water to keep cool. Mothers may be washing their clothes, but we will not disturb them. We will lie on the cool sand in the shade of the palm trees."

They splashed in the water at the edge of the pond, took a cool drink from the spring, and then went up the path to the mud hut with the thatched roof. Mo noticed that dark clouds were coming up in the western sky.

"I know this is not the rainy season, little Dookie, but I hope it rains. The ground is dry and hard." He placed the baby on the mat, and she smiled up at him, waving her small brown hands as if she knew what he was talking about.

"Yes, the rice and bean crops could stand a good rain," he said as he began preparing rice for his supper.

Suddenly the wind began to blow. Twigs and leaves whirled around the house and came in at the open door. When the bamboo gate fell down with a thud, little Dookie was frightened. She threw up her little hands and cried. Big Mo picked her up and spoke words of comfort in her tiny brown ears. From somewhere in the distance came the threatening roll of thunder. Soon big drops of rain fell on the dusty ground.

42

The child had not seen rain before, and her eyes grew wide with fear
and uncertainty. He held her close and took her away from the doorway.

"See!" said Mo, holding Dookie so she could watch the rain. "Look at the rain! Nice rain. Good rain."

The child had not seen rain before, and her eyes grew wide with fear and uncertainty. When she clutched at Mo's arm and trembled, he held her close and took her away from the doorway.

"It is only the thunder spirits, little one," he said. "They send the big thunder that comes with the rain. Do not be afraid." But even as he tried to comfort her, his own heart was filled with fear. The lightning flashed vividly, the thunder crashed and rumbled loudly, and the wind seemed to vent its fury on the mud hut. The edges of the thatch on the roof flapped back and forth, and rain blew in through the open door. Mo took the sleeping mat from the floor and put it on a shelf near the roof. He knew that the foundation of his house was firm, for he had built it with his own strong hands. He had used large rocks, firmly embedded in the ground. The thatch had been securely fastened with strong fiber cords. He believed that the roof would not blow away; yet he was not too sure!

Big Mo had been in storms before, but some-how this one was different. This time he was really frightened, though he could not tell why. Could it be that the thunder spirits were angry with him? For what reason? He could think of none. He had given a generous gift of money to the charm doctor for Spindlelegs and little Doo-

44

kie. Many times he had placed flowers on the shrine. Where had he failed?

Tiny brown hands clutched his arm more tightly each time the thunder crashed. Mo rocked the little girl gently in his arms as he walked around the room, trying to calm her fears and also his own.

Dookie cried out in fear at each loud clap of thunder. His own fears subsided somewhat as he thought of the utter helplessness of the little one in his arms. The spirits could not be angry with her; she had never done anything wrong. It was not her fault that she was a girl.

"Do not cry, my precious one," said Mo. "This is only a bad storm. Whoever makes the rain must be a powerful god. I wish I knew who makes the rain," he said, more to himself than to Dookie. "Perhaps I will know someday."

At last the rain stopped and the storm passed. Mo gave little Dookie her supper, adding some rice water to the milk and honey. The baby was growing, and she needed more food.

When the chores were all done and it was time to go to bed, Mo found a dry spot on the floor, where he laid the sleeping mat and stretched out beside the sleeping Dookie.

"Someday I will know," said Mo again as he listened to the night sounds. He saw big clouds sailing across the sky, hiding the stars and moon. As he watched them he whispered softly, "Someday I'll know who makes the rain!"

45

Mo leaped to his feet and ran down the stony path toward the village. Dookie stopped crying and looked up at him. This was unexpected.

Flowers for the Spirits

LITTLE Dookie was growing bigger every day. No father was ever more devoted to a daughter than was Big Mo to the little girl. He played with her, and laughed with her, and talked and sang to her. In turn she smiled and laughed for him, clung to him, and depended on him. During the long evenings Mo spent much time carving little wooden dolls for her to play with. They were queer creations with funny faces, but Dookie thought they were wonderful.

One day as she sat on the floor playing with a coconut, it slipped from her hands and rolled across the floor. She looked at it for a moment, then rolled over on her stomach and started to go after it. Mo took a step to help her, but then he stopped. Like little Spindlelegs, she must learn to help herself.

Keeping her eyes on the coconut, Dookie wiggled and worked her way across the floor until she could touch the big oval with her hand. Then it rolled on a little farther. Dookie put her head down on the floor; she was disappointed because she had failed.

"Try again, little one," said Mo gently. "You can do it. Rest a little and then try again."

Dookie looked up into Mo's face and smiled. She tried again and soon recovered the coconut. With a smile of triumph on her little brown face, she held the coconut firmly in both hands.

"Good girl," said Mo, praising her for her efforts. "You did it all by yourself!"

For many days Mo watched Dookie's efforts to crawl. Then one morning something happened that caused Big Mo concern. While Dookie was interested in her toys and dolls on the mat, Mo stepped out the door for a few moments. When he returned he found that Dookie had crawled over to the fireplace in the corner where the kettle of rice was cooking. The little girl saw a few grains of rice on the edge of the kettle, and with her little brown hand she was reaching for them. In order to steady herself, she put the other hand down on one of the hot stones, and it burned her!

At that moment Mo came in the door. Seeing what was happening, he said, "No, no, Dookie. Hot, hot!"

The shock of the burn and the quick, harsh

words of the only person she knew and loved, were more than the little girl could take. Her lips quivered, her eyes looked up searchingly into Big Mo's face, and then she put her head on the floor between her hands and sobbed. The burn on her hand hurt, of course; but what hurt more was that Big Mo had used a harsh tone of voice to her. She could not understand.

Mo gathered her up in his arms and looked at her hand. It was not a bad burn. While he applied some oil, he spoke words of tenderness to her. Then he sat on the mat and held her close to him. He sang to her, but she continued to sob. When she looked up at his face there was fear and distrust in her eyes. Mo had not intended to scold her. He had not wanted any harm to come to her; he loved her so much! Then a sudden fear came to him like the stab of a knife. What if the spirits were angry and would take her away from him because he had scolded her?

With a suddenness that startled Dookie, Mo leaped to his feet. Taking some coins from the jar on the shelf, he ran down the stony path toward the village. Dookie stopped crying and looked up at him questioningly. This was strange and unexpected. Where were they going so fast?

When they came to the village Mo hurried to the market and bought a large bouquet of flowers. Then he ran back across the clearing to the spirit tree near the road. On the shrine he placed the flowers, mumbling the queer incantations of the charm doctor, as he stood there afraid and sorrowful. Dookie held out her small hand. She wanted the pretty flowers. Why leave them there? Big Mo held her close as he walked slowly back up the hill path. He breathed a big sigh; he hoped he had appeased the spirits.

"I'll never scold her again," he promised. "Never, never!"

Dookie had forgotten all about the hurt. The fast ride to the village and the pretty flowers had made her trouble disappear. Even the burn on her hand did not hurt any more, for she was assured that Big Mo still loved her.

Trinkets and Charms

THE sun was peering over the palm trees across the silver river when Big Mo finished his chores. Dookie was still asleep on the mat on the floor. Suddenly a shadow fell across the square patch of light in the open doorway, and Mo turned to face the charm doctor!

He was not a big man in stature, but he was great in the eyes of the villagers, for he calmed the spirits and revoked the curses by the use of his trinkets and charms. (At least it seemed so in most cases.) On his head he wore his ceremonial headdress made of long hair, beads, bones, and shells interwoven in a weird design. The markings on his face made him look bold and fierce. Strings of shells and tiny bones hung from his neck and arms. His garment was embroidered with bright-colored threads, with beads and trinkets attached. He wore a pair of sandals on his feet, for he was the spirit medium for the higher-caste people, as well as for the lower-caste. The higher-caste were permitted to wear shoes.

"Good morning," said Mo. "You startled me for a moment. I did not see you coming."

The charm doctor edged into the room and looked around.

"Nice, nice," he said. "You are a rich man. You have five nice cows, too, and a good rice crop. You are, indeed, a rich man. But I have come to make you richer. There is a big man over in the village beyond the three hills that challenges you to a fight at the time you say. He is a big man, and will give you a good fight; but I know you can beat him. What do you say? He asked me to make the arrangements; that is why I came this morning."

"No," said Big Mo, shaking his head as he looked down at the little sleeper on the mat. "I'm not interested."

"But if it is the little one you are thinking about, someone in the crowd will hold her for you. There is quite a bit of money involved in this fight."

Again Mo shook his head. "No," he said, with finality in his voice.

The charm doctor was not easily shaken. He patted his money bag and said with a sly, knowing gleam in his eyes, "I have ways to make you the winner."

"But I will not fight that way," said Big Mo. "I fight with my own strength in a fair way. I do not need your money bad enough for you to fix a fight."

There was a moment of silence. Then the charm doctor pointed his long, bony finger down at the sleeping baby, saying, "Then this will have to go! It is this child that is keeping you from doing the things you did before—the fights, the money you received for yourself and for the spirits."

As Big Mo stood up straight and tall, he looked down into the evil eyes of the charm doctor. Mo was unafraid as he said, "She will stay with me as long as I have the strength to keep her. As I told you before, she is a gift to me from the spirits. I will guard her with my life." Then, as if to dismiss the subject, Mo took down the big gourd from the peg in the corner, and poured some drink into a coconut shell and silently handed it to the charm doctor.

"I see you are a good host," said the charm doctor. "You do not forget your hospitality." As he faced the big man of the village, he spoke words of flattery in order not to antagonize him.

"Good," he said over and over, as Mo poured him another drink.

"If you wish, you may take the rest with you," said Mo. "The gourd is about two thirds full.

The charm doctor gazed at her with evil eyes. He shook his chain of bones and shells, and pointed his bony finger at her. Dookie screamed.

Yes, take the gourd with you. I will not need it any more."

The eyes of the charm doctor lighted up with pleasure as he accepted the gift. He looked down at the sleeping child on the floor and said, "When she is older, she will come to the temple, perhaps?"

"To the temple!" Mo shouted out the words in anger. "Never will I take her to the temple. She is mine to raise as my daughter, and I will teach her to be a fine lady, to be respected by everyone. She is *mine,* I tell you, my gift from the spirits! Let nobody ever try to take her from me!"

The sound of loud voices awakened Dookie and she looked up at the two men standing and talking angrily above her. The charm doctor gazed down at her with evil eyes. He shook his chain of bones and shells, and pointed his bony finger at her. When Dookie screamed in fright, Big Mo quickly took her up and held her close. She put her little arms around his neck, and cuddled up to get away from the charm doctor.

"Please go," said Mo. "Can't you see that you frighten her?"

The charm doctor picked up the gourd and went out the door, saying, "You will feel the curse of snakes because of this. You will see!" With rapid steps he went out the door and down the path.

For a long time Dookie clung to Big Mo's

neck, her body trembling with fear. He patted her gently and walked around the room, speaking words of assurance and comfort to her. Then suddenly he remembered the day she burned her hand on the hot stone in the fireplace. How quickly the run to the village made her forget her fears.

"Shall we go to the flower market in the village and get some flowers?" he asked. Dookie looked at him and smiled through her tears. Away they went down the hill path to the village. Mo had somehow expected to overtake the charm doctor, but he was nowhere to be seen. He was not at the shrine when Mo took the bouquet of flowers as an offering. Then back up the hill they went. Little Dookie laughed with joy as Mo carried her on his broad shoulders.

The Patter of Little Feet

IT WAS the time of the rice harvest, when the days were busy for the big man of the village. Little Dookie sat on her blanket out in the field watching Big Mo as he threshed the kernels of rice from the rice straw. She watched him pick the bean pods and thresh out the little round beans. When the sun was high, Big Mo would pause from his work to eat his noon meal. The little girl ate some of the soft grains of cooked rice and drank the milk from her small gourd.

"You are growing so big, Dookie," said Mo, smiling proudly. "Soon you will learn to walk and talk and sing, and do so many other things little girls do. You must learn to be a fine lady someday. I will be so proud of you, my little gift of the spirits."

Then one day Dookie took her first steps alone. How it thrilled Mo when she came to him as he held out his hands to her! Sometimes she would lose her balance and fall, but he would encourage her by saying, "Steady, little girl. Spindlelegs did it. You can do it, too."

Seasons came and went; the harvest was good. Soon came the time for planting again. Heavy rains flooded the paddy fields. Mo built up the bund, the mud-and-stone wall around the edge of the field to keep in the water. Little Dookie liked to play in the water. She squealed with delight when she sat on the edge of the bund and sent the spray flying.

In the evenings as Mo and Dookie sat in the doorway watching the firelight, or waited for the big moon to rise over the palm trees, they spent many pleasant hours learning words.

"What's that?" asked Dookie, pointing to the moon.

"That is the moon," said Mo. He told her all about the trees, the jungle grass, the night birds that called to each other in the darkness. He told her about the stars that twinkled in the sky above. He wondered, as he looked up at the numberless stars, if there were spirits that lived on them, or if someone made them and put them up there to be lights to shine at night.

"What's that?" asked Dookie, pointing to the fire.

"That is fire. It would burn my little one."

Then he held her close and his voice was low and tender. He remembered the day when she burned her hand on the hot stone of the fireplace.

It was surprising how quickly Dookie learned new words. What a jolly time they had playing "Get me." Mo would get down on the floor and pat-pat after her when she challenged him, "Get me!" Away she would patter across the hard floor on her bare feet with Big Mo after her. Yes, life was full of happiness for both of them.

When they went to the spring for water, there were tiny footprints in the moist sand beside the big ones.

"See," said Dookie. "Big feet and little feet. Big feet, Big Mo's. Little feet, Dookie's." Then she would laugh.

Mo did the family washing in the pond and dried the garments on nearby bushes. Dookie splashed in the water close beside him. Sometimes there were other children playing in the water not far off, and she watched them with interest. "Boys, girls," she would say, "play in the water."

Sometimes the children ventured near to play with Dookie; but Big Mo always kept a watchful eye, lest they play too rough and accidentally harm her. He knew she would be happy playing with other children, for their merry laughter revealed their pleasure. Someday she would be a big girl, and then she would choose her own companions. She must go to school to learn many things he could not teach her. He wanted her to be a fine lady, respected by everyone. He wanted only the best for the girl, for she was very precious to him.

One night as Mo and Dookie sat before the fire, watching the moon come up, she asked, "Big Mo, why don't I have a mother?"

For a moment the man did not know what to say. He looked silently into the fire as though seeking for words to explain the situation. Dookie noticed the silence and asked, "What is a mother?"

Mo took her on his lap and said, "Haven't I been a good mother to you? Haven't I done my best to fill the place of both a father and a mother? When you came, my whole life changed. There were no more fights and no more drinking from the big gourd. My life is only for you, little one. What more would you ask from me?" Then in answer to her inquiries he began to tell her about the mother cow and Spindlelegs, who was now as big as her mother. Then he reminded her that birds built nests in the trees, that the mother birds laid eggs in the nests and watched over them, and soon baby birds hatched for the mother and father birds to feed and protect. He called to mind the chickens that scratched for seeds and crumbs in the road. She had seen them many times following the mother hen.

"The big, cross hen—is she the mother?" asked Dookie.

60

"Yes," said Mo.

"Then I do not want a mother; I just want you." The girl snuggled against his shoulder and patted his cheek with her warm hand.

Dookie was full of questions. "Did I have a cross mother? And did you take me away from her so she would not hurt me?"

"No, little one, your mother was not a cross mother. She was kind, and she loved you very much. You also had a father, but he died of the fever about the time you were born."

"Why did he leave my mother then?" asked Dookie. "Didn't he know she would need him to help take care of me?"

"It was the spirits," said Mo. "They were very angry when they took him away. Then something strange happened. Instead of letting a terrible thing happen to you, the spirits brought you to me. That is why I call you my gift from the spirits."

"Did you ever see my father?"

"I might have seen him at the markets, but I did not know him."

"Did you ever see my mother?"

"Yes, I saw her once. Her name was Resa."

"Do you think she loved me?" asked Dookie, looking wistfully into Mo's face.

"Yes, little one, I know she loved you, for she held you against her cheek. As she placed you in my arms, she said, 'Please, will you keep her for me? Will you take care of her and be kind to

61

her?' I promised that I would. I have never seen her since. So you see, little Dookie, I have been both father and mother to you."

"Then there are just the two of us?" asked Dookie.

"Yes, just the two of us," said Mo.

Luani

MONG the children that played with Dookie at the pond was an older girl named Luani. Mo noticed her devotion and fondness for his little girl, as though she were a sister. Luani was always sharing toys with Dookie, seeking her comfort, and being fair with her in all their games. Luani seemed different from the other boys and girls who played at the pond while their mothers washed clothes.

One day while Dookie and Luani were making mud balls at the edge of the pond, Luani asked, "Dookie, when you come to the spring, why doesn't your mother come, too?"

"I do not have a mother," replied Dookie. "Big Mo is all the mother I have. He cares for me and loves me. He even washes my clothes!" Both girls laughed, because it was unusual for men to do the work of women.

"Would you like to see my mother?" asked Luani.

"Is she a cross mother?" asked Dookie.

"No, she is not cross. She is a good mother. Shall we ask Big Mo if you may go with me to see my mother? She is washing clothes over there on the rocks."

"Yes," said Dookie, "I really would like to see your mother."

Brushing the sand from their hands and knees, Luani and Dookie ran to where Big Mo was washing garments and milk strainers. He looked up and smiled as the two girls came near.

"May I go with Luani to see her mother?"

Luani hurried to explain, "You see, Dookie doesn't have any mother but you. May she come with me to see my mother? She is not a cross mother; she likes to talk to little girls."

"Where is your mother?" asked Mo.

"Right over there, washing out our clothes," said Luani, pointing in the direction of a woman who was kneeling on a rock, dipping a garment up and down in the water.

Mo thought it might be wise for Dookie to meet a mother, since she had become curious about her own. Since Luani was such a kind, thoughtful playmate, surely the mother would be kind, also.

"You may go for just a little while," said Mo.

Luani and Dookie ran to where Big Mo was washing garments and milk strainers. The man looked up and smiled as the two girls came near.

A look of anticipated pleasure crossed the girl's face.

"I will come back to you soon," Dookie said.
"You will not go home without me, will you?"

"I'll wait right here for you," he promised.

The two girls pattered along the wet sand to see Luani's mother. Dookie was shy at first, for she had never talked to a mother before. She timidly dug her toes in the sand as she looked at the woman carefully, noting the long, dark hair pulled back in a roll at the neck, the kind eyes, the friendly smile, the feminine softness of the throat and arms, and the neatly arranged sari that she wore.

So this was a mother! She had seen many women at a distance carrying their babies on their hips, or washing clothes at the pond. Somehow Mo always managed to avoid meeting them face to face, and the women always kept out of his way. They were not anxious to be near the big man of the village.

"Do not be afraid of me, child," said the mother kindly. "I would like to be your friend. Luani tells me you are a bright child. Where do you go to school?"

"I do not go to school," said Dookie. "There is no need for me to go because, you see, when we sit by the fire at night and watch the moon come up, Big Mo teaches me what I need to know. There are so many things I must learn so I can grow up to be a fine lady."

"He has taught you well," said Luani's mother. "I am sure he is proud of you, for you are a fine little lady now."

The woman was surprised that the child could answer her questions with such intelligence. Big Mo had been a good father, in spite of the reports of the villagers.

After the two girls had talked to the mother for several minutes, Dookie suddenly remembered her promise to Big Mo. "I think he is ready to go now. I am glad I could talk to a real mother. I'll come to see you again sometime. Good-by."

That night as Big Mo and Dookie sat on the doorstep, she asked him a question that made the strong man of the village tremble with fear. She could feel the muscles in the strong arm around her quiver and tighten as she waited for his answer. She repeated her question, thinking perhaps that he had not heard the first time.

"May I go to the mission school with Luani?"

Big Mo put his arm more firmly around her as he said huskily, "Oh, my precious girl, what have I done? The spirits will really be angry. They might even take you from me."

"Why?" asked Dookie, looking into his face.

"Because the mission-school people are Christians."

"Christians?" echoed Dookie. "What are Christians? You never told me about Christians before."

"I did not tell you about Christians before because I thought I could keep you away from them until you were big enough to understand how dangerous they are. Do you remember that long walk we took one day when we followed the bees to see if we could find their hive? We came to some long white buildings with red roofs?"

"You mean the temple?" she asked.

"No, we saw the temple that day, too. But the mission is beyond the village at the end of the winding road."

"Yes, I remember. You told me we would not go any closer because that was where the Christians were, and we should not talk to them."

"That is right," said Mo. "You remember well."

"But what do Christians do to you?" asked Dookie.

"Even if you talk to them they cast a spell over you, and this angers the spirits. How could I know that Luani and her mother were Christians?"

"I don't think Christians are so bad," said Dookie. "Luani is my friend, and her mother was very kind to me. She wouldn't cast a spell over me, would she?"

Big Mo flipped a little rock into the fire before he answered. "That is what is so puzzling. Luani is a kind little girl, and I thought you were safe when you played with her. But one never knows."

Dookie put her arms around Mo's neck and

cuddled against his shoulder. "They won't cast a spell over me; I won't let them."

"Hush, my little one. Let us not boast about things over which we have no control. There are many dangers to fear in the big world: tigers, bears, leopards, and wild dogs. There are curses of the spirits, curses of snakes, curses of the devil gods, curses of fire, flood, and wind. But the spell of the Christians is the most to be feared. They are tricky, for they fool us with their gentle ways, and before we know it, we become Christians, too. Then the spirits come upon us with terrible curses! My little one, they might even take you away from me. What can we do?"

For a long time Mo held her close. He was thinking hard. Then an idea came to him: flowers, yes, flowers for the little shrine under the spirit tree!

"We will go to the village early in the morning and get many flowers for the spirits," he said, jumping up quickly. "But now we will put up the bamboo gate and go to sleep."

As Dookie started back to the house, she tripped over something lying across her path. Scrambling to her feet, she ran to the house crying.

The Little Rope

EARLY the next morning Big Mo and Dookie hurried down the path toward the village. The old man had not yet set up his flower stand in the market; but when he heard the jingle of the coins in Mo's hand, he came hobbling around the corner with a toothless grin on his wrinkled face. "Nice flowers," he said, "nice flowers to give to the little one."

"But these are not for the little one," said Mo. "These are for the shrine."

"Yes," the old man nodded understandingly, for Mo had made many similar purchases. "To be sure; for the spirit shrine."

Mo selected a large bouquet and dropped a handful of coins into the aged hand.

"This is too much money," said the flower seller. "I do not ask for so many coins."

71

"This is a special gift for the spirits, a very special gift." And before the old man could say more, Big Mo and Dookie and the flowers were across the street.

Dookie thought it was a shame to leave the pretty flowers where nobody could see them and enjoy them. But the same thing had happened many times before. She wondered what the spirits did with them. Surely they didn't eat the flowers—or did they? They were always gone the next time they came. They were too pretty to lie there and wither.

Dookie asked many questions as they walked home, but Mo only said, "Hush, little one, the spirits may already be angry. Do not provoke them, lest something terrible come upon us."

When they arrived home, they found that Kola had come for the cows. As usual, he spoke but few words. He liked Mo, but there was a certain reckless attitude about the big man that Kola could not understand. He was certainly a good father. How tenderly he cared for Dookie. How faithfully he guarded her from danger.

"Wait, Kola," said Dookie, as the youth started driving the cows toward the grasslands. "I will walk with you as far as the path."

"Did you ask Big Mo?" said Kola.

"Yes, I asked him, and he said I might go if I came right back."

"All right," said Kola, urging the slow-moving cows before him.

72

"That lazy Spindlelegs," said Dookie, with a merry laugh. "She is always the last one in line, isn't she?"

Kola smiled at the little girl beside him. "Yes," he said, "but she is always the first one to start home at night."

When they came to the rough path, Dookie said, "I must go back now, Kola, but I will watch you until you and the cows are down by the big rocks. Take good care of yourself and the cows. Good-by!"

As Dookie started back to the house, she tripped over something that was lying across her path. She scrambled to her feet and ran to the house crying.

"What happened, little one?" asked Big Mo, coming to meet her. "What happened to cause all these tears?"

"I fell down," she sobbed. "I tripped over that rope down by the big bush."

"But you are a big girl now," said Mo, patting her shoulder. "Big girls do not cry like this when they stumble and fall over a piece of rope."

"But I hurt my leg on that rope when I fell."

"What rope?" asked Mo. "I didn't know there was a rope—"

"Right over there by that bush." She pointed in the direction.

"Rope?" Mo took big strides to the bush and came running back for his hatchet. The "rope" was a deadly snake!

With a strong blow Mo killed the snake, and then he hurried back to Dookie. He examined the hurt, and realized he had nothing in the house with which to treat it. He had some oil, but the poison from the snake would not be affected by the oil. He needed something much stronger. If only he had some liquor in the big gourd; but he had given all of it to the charm doctor. With a sickening heart he noted the leg was swelling and becoming red. He realized that the curse of the snakes had come much quicker than he had expected—in spite of the flowers on the shrine!

"Oh, my little one!" he said, gathering her in his arms. "It should not come to you, for you are so young and good. I will take you at once to the charm doctor. We must hurry!"

"It was that Christian mother," Mo kept repeating to himself as he hurried down the street to the charm doctor. "I should never have let Dookie go to see the woman."

The charm doctor seemed to be in no hurry to examine the unconscious child in Big Mo's arms. He mumbled weird incantations as he mixed a potion of ashes and brown liquid in an earthen bowl. Then he applied the mixture around the wound, on the bottoms of her feet, and on her forehead. He made ceremonial gestures, bowing and waving his arms in rhythm to his chanting, and dancing up and down on his toes.

Big Mo listened and watched, hoping to see signs that the charms or the medicine was working. This went on for what seemed hours, but the swelling increased, and the child tossed and moaned in an unconscious condition.

"Is this all you can do?" Mo finally asked. "She seems to be getting worse instead of better."

"If you will remember," said the charm doctor, "I told you a long time ago that the curse of snakes would come to you because you refused to take her to the temple. Now it has come, as you can see for yourself."

"But isn't there something I can do? I cannot let her suffer this way. I will do anything!"

"Take her to the spirit tree. That is where she was taken from as a baby. Lay her on the shrine and go away. Only then will she be all right. Now go at once, and I will drink from the big gourd and call off the curse of the spirits."

"I will go," said Mo meekly, but there was a look of distrust on his face. He carried little Dookie toward the spirit shrine. Gently he laid her on the stones, and then sobbed bitterly.

"Oh, my little gift of the spirits, now I must give you back to them. But I just can't leave you here to die! There must be some other way."

How long Mo lay there under the spirit tree, he did not know. He could not leave Dookie, for she was his life. There was no need to go home; she would not be there. Suddenly he was aroused by a noise beside him. He looked up to see a man standing above him.

Big Mo gripped the doctor with both hands. "Is she dead? Tell me, is she dead? If you have killed her, I will crush the life out of you."

The Woodcutter's Advice

"CAN I help you?" the man asked kindly, as he took a bundle of wood from his head. "I was passing with my bundle of wood and I saw you here. Is there anything I can do for you?"

"If you only could help me," said Mo.

"What has happened to the little girl?" he asked.

Mo showed him. "See the snake bite? It is the curse of the snakes! The spirits are angry."

The woodcutter examined the wound closely. "It is a bad one," he said, shaking his head; "but I think there is still hope."

"Tell me what to do," begged Mo. "I can't leave her here to die. I will do anything to save this child from the curse of snakes."

77

"First of all," said the woodcutter, "I do not believe in the curse of snakes or any of the false superstitions of the Savaras. I can see no help in the methods of treatment used by the charm doctor. I would, first, wash off the manure and ashes with clean water, and then take her to the mission hospital as fast as you can. The man at the mission has wonderful magic for snake bites."

"The mission!" echoed Mo in unbelief. Yet in his mind there seemed to be one flickering light of hope. "Are you sure?"

The woodcutter had an honest face. Surely he would not lie to him about so serious a matter.

"Yes," said the woodcutter, "I am sure. But I would hurry if I were you. There is no time to lose. Now is there anything I can do for you—cows to milk, perhaps, while you are gone?"

Suddenly Mo remembered the milk in the jars at home, ready to be taken to the village. "If you will take the milk to the village for me, I will pay you well. Kola takes care of the cows." Quickly he gave the woodcutter a few instructions and then started toward the pond with Dookie in his arms.

Mo washed off the brown mixture of ashes and manure that the charm doctor had applied. He bathed the girl's feverish face and arms in cool water, and then he started through the village toward the Christian mission.

Mo thought of the kind woodcutter's words:

"Wonderful magic for snake bites—no time to lose." It was a long way to the white buildings with red-tiled roofs. It was against his belief to go near the mission; but in this case, when he had tried everything he knew, he would defy the charm doctor. He would defy all the spirits and devil gods. He would risk all the curses that they might put upon him if he could only save the precious little one he carried in his arms.

People looked at him curiously as he hurried along. Dogs barked and chickens squawked as he made his way along the street. Skinny cats scuttled under bushes to get out of the path.

The hot rays of the sun beat down upon him, but he did not seem to notice. Usually at that time of day the people of the village rested in the shade, but Mo did not take time to rest. It was a long way up the winding road. He was weary and his muscles ached as perspiration ran down his forehead and back. When he reached the mission, a kind lady met him at the door and listened to his story.

"If the doctor will only help her with his wonderful magic for snake bites! I can't let the spirits take her from me. She is very dear to me."

When the mission doctor arrived, he quickly gave orders to put the girl in the emergency room.

"I will do all I can for her," said the doctor to Mo. "But you must first understand that I can do nothing of myself. It is only with the aid of the Great Physician, the God in heaven, that I can achieve results."

"But," began Mo, "the woodcutter said you had magic—wonderful magic for snake bites. That is why I brought her here!"

"I understand, and I appreciate your confidence in me. It has taken a lot of courage to come here, for I know the attitude of the Savaras toward the mission."

Tactfully the doctor talked to Mo as he treated the snake bite. He asked and answered many questions. Big Mo stood by, watching, yet helpless in such a time.

The doctor was not a big man, yet he seemed well able to care for those who came to him for help. Mo noticed the man's high forehead, his hair graying at the temples, his kind eyes behind the glasses, the dexterity of the hands as they worked on the little patient. Mo noticed that the doctor had slippers on his feet; this indicated that the doctor must be high-caste, for only high-caste people were permitted to wear shoes.

The mission lady gently bathed the face of the unconscious girl. Then Mo listened silently as the doctor prayed to the great God in heaven. The mission lady bowed her head reverently, too. It was a simple prayer of faith and trust, asking the Giver of life to restore health to the little one and take away the poison that had come into her body.

There was no wild waving of hands, no danc-

80

ing of feet, no chanting in rhythm to rattling strings of bones and shells. After the prayer, Big Mo watched the doctor use the magic needle with the magic water that cured snake bites. The doctor explained to Mo how it worked.

"Will it not hurt her to put the needle in her leg?" Mo asked anxiously.

"Does she see you with her eyes when you talk to her? Does she hear with her ears?"

Mo shook his head.

"Then she will not feel the needle."

Mo watched the magic water disappear out of the glass tube. "You have done well in raising the little girl," said the doctor. "She is clean, strong, and healthy. The medicine can work much better because her heart is strong and she has good blood."

Big Mo looked down at Dookie. She was no longer tossing and moaning. She lay still on the white bed. Suddenly Mo leaned forward, gripped the doctor on the shoulders with both hands, and said, "Is she dead? Tell me, is she dead? If you have killed her, I will crush the life out of you with my bare hands."

He said no more, for as he looked into the eyes of the mission doctor, something melted within Mo. His hands became limp and dropped to his sides. Fear clutched his heart, for he had dared to touch a Christian! Still there was something in the eyes of the kind doctor that commanded respect and sympathy and love.

"My friend, she is only sleeping," said the doctor. "The medicine is doing its work. Listen and hear her heart beating. Notice the even, normal breathing. When she wakes, she will talk to you as she did before it happened."

Mo looked anxiously at Dookie. With all his heart he wanted to believe that the doctor was right. "Are you sure?" he said huskily. "It is not a trick?"

"Touch her and see for yourself," said the doctor.

Mo touched her face, and watched the rise and fall of the girl's chest in the regular rhythm of normal breathing. He was satisfied. "I will pay you whatever you ask," he said gratefully. "I'll sell my cows. I will work for you, do anything. She means everything to me, for she is all I have."

"We will talk about the pay at a later time. Just now, while we wait for the reaction of the magic water, let us sit here and talk as brothers."

Mo agreed. It would be good to rest, for he was tired.

"You are a good father, Mo," began the doctor. "I can see that you love her very much. Now let me tell you about the great God in heaven. He is our heavenly Father, and we are His children —you and I, and this precious girl. He loves each one of us even more than you could possibly love that little one. He watches over us, guards us, and protects us from harm. Sometimes He permits things to happen to us in order that we will change our ways. For example, this snake bite: Would you have come to me for help if you had not, as a last resort, realized there was no other help? You see, God wanted you to come to the hospital so you could learn of His great love for you. Do you now understand why it happened and why it is not a curse of the spirits? The heavenly Father wants us to come to Him with all our troubles. He would take us in His loving arms and comfort us, as you do this little girl. His love is so much greater than ours, even as your strength is greater than that of this little girl. Think it over, my friend; it is worthy of your consideration."

The mission lady sat on a chair near the bed. "Everything will be all right," she said softly. "Please, for her sake, try to get some rest."

The Long Night

THE mission lady and Neda, one of the nurses, brought in a tray of food for Big Mo and the doctor as they sat on stools watching for signs of definite change in the little girl.

Big Mo ate heartily, for he was hungry. He had not thought of food in his hours of anxiety. The mission lady made sure there was plenty for the visitor to eat.

The doctor asked Mo many questions during the night of watching, and the big man, in turn, asked many questions which the doctor was glad to answer. Mo was getting a far different idea of Christians. He learned that they were good, that they did not cast a spell over you. They believed in the great and powerful God of heaven, the Creator of all things. The doctor read from a black-covered Book called the Bible. There were gold letters on the cover, so it must be true, thought Mo.

Finally the doctor closed the Book and said, "There are many precious promises in this Book for us if we will accept them. But now, you are tired. It has been a long, hard day. Shall we go and rest a little while? The mission lady will watch the little girl while we get some rest."

The doctor offered to let Mo sleep on a cot in the next room, but Mo said, "No, thank you. You are very kind. But suppose she should wake up in this strange place and be frightened? Would you permit me to stretch out here on the floor by the bed, just in case she wakes up and needs me?"

"Of course; I should have thought of that. I will bring you a blanket," said the physician.

With a sigh, Mo stretched out on the floor by the bed. The doctor turned out the light, leaving the room in darkness but for the rays that shone in from the hall lights. The mission lady came and sat on a chair near the bed.

"Everything will be all right," she said softly. "Please, for her sake, try to get some rest. She will need you when she wakes up."

Big Mo closed his eyes, and because he was physically tired, he quickly fell asleep. Many times he stirred and mumbled, "My precious girl." Then he awoke suddenly and looked around, in a bewildered manner.

The mission lady was still sitting by the bed. She smiled reassuringly and said, "The girl is going to be all right. We can thank the loving heavenly Father, who does so much for us. Try to get some more sleep. I will keep watch over your little one. If she needs you, I will awaken you."

Pink Dawn

BIG Mo stirred, stretched his muscular arms, and sat up. The mission lady was still sitting by the bed. When Mo sprang to his feet, he saw Dookie on the bed, sleeping normally. Gently he touched her cheek with his rough hand. She stirred lightly; she was still alive! The magic had worked. The woodcutter was right; it was wonderful magic for snake bites. Then he remembered how the doctor had said that without the help of the God in heaven all the efforts he could make would be in vain.

From the window, Mo saw the pink dawn lighting up the eastern sky. Birds were singing in the trees on the mission compound. The words of the doctor and the mission lady were stirring in his confused mind. He wanted to believe what they had told him, yet years of superstition could not be changed in a single night. Mo broke the silence in the room by saying, "Kind lady, may I ask you a question?"

"Yes," she said, not knowing what his request might be.

"There is one thing I have wondered about for a long time: Did the God in heaven that made the sun, moon, and stars, also make the rain?"

She had not expected such an easy question, for Big Mo was a man of intelligence. "Yes, the God in heaven is the Creator of all the universe," said the woman. "He makes the lakes, the rivers, and the springs of water. He sends the rain to give a drink to the thirsty grasslands and rice fields. He puts life into those little birds you hear twittering in the trees. He is the great Life-giver, who gives life to all the animals and people on the earth. Contrary to what you have been taught to believe, and what the people of your village say, it was the God in heaven, not the spirits, who gave you the little girl. He will keep back the evil spirits so they cannot harm her, if you trust in Him. When you are in trouble you may call upon Him, and He will help you. Have I answered your question?"

"Yes, thank you," said Mo. He touched the little hand of the sleeping child, and again she stirred. It thrilled him that she had responded to his slightest touch. Mo watched her even breathing for a few minutes. Then he went outside to enjoy the fresh morning air, and to watch the glorious sunrise. Many new thoughts were racing through his mind, for a new hope was awakening inside him. There was a new God to thank, to trust, to serve. How much he owed to this wonderful God who made the world, the trees, the rain, and everything about him. Most of all, He had given Mo his precious little girl. He had so much to tell her when she awoke, so much to tell her about God.

The Broken Promise

ONE of the nurses, coming on duty for the day shift, saw Big Mo standing near the building watching the sun rise. She remembered he was the man who yesterday brought a little girl to the hospital with a snake bite.

From the window of the building she watched Mo as he went back into the hospital. Something still puzzled her: Where had she seen him before? All through the day she tried to remember. Then it flashed into her mind: The tiny baby wrapped in a light blanket, the spirit shrine, the house on the hill—could it be the same? Hastily putting the pile of linens on the shelf, the nurse went and asked to speak to the mission lady.

"Are you sure it is Big Mo?" she asked. "The child—the little girl—may I see her?"

The lady noted the excitement, the expectancy in the nurse's manner. "Of course you may see her," said the lady. "She is asleep, but her daddy is watching over her, waiting for her to wake up."

"Oh," said the nurse, "I couldn't go in there now, not when he is in there. I promised I would never see the child again. But I must see her! She is my own little girl!"

The lady put her arm around the nurse and said, "Sit down, Resa, and tell me about it. I would like to hear the whole story, if you would care to tell me."

The nurse told her story from the very beginning. "But I am a Christian now," said Resa, "and I no longer believe in the spirits and their curses. Would it be right for me to break my promise and see my little girl? Would it be right?"

"Because you know now the spirits no longer have control over those who put their trust in the God in heaven, I see no reason why you should be held to that promise," said the lady. "But, on the other hand, Big Mo might not understand. He has gone through so much for the girl, perhaps it would be better for him if you wait for a time. Soon he will go to the dining room for breakfast. You may look in and see her then. Or I can send a note with him to the doctor right now, if you wish. The doctor will keep him busy for a few minutes."

Resa wondered what her eyes were like. She leaned over and kissed the warm forehead. "I wish she might learn to love Jesus," she whispered.

"Thank you," said Resa, as she went back to her duties. Anxiously she waited, her heart beating rapidly. The mission lady soon stood at the door, beckoning her. She hesitated a moment. "Are you sure it is not wrong for me to see her?" asked Resa. "I do want to see my little girl. My heart still loves her, though we are strangers."

"Come," urged the lady. "I am sure it is all right. Let us go to her bed."

Tears came into Resa's eyes as she looked down at the sleeping child. Very gently she touched the little one's hair, her small brown hand, her soft cheek. Resa wondered what her eyes were like, how her voice sounded. All the wondering and longing of the past few years welled up within her. She leaned over and kissed the warm forehead.

"How I wish that she might learn to love Jesus, too!" Resa whispered.

"It will come in time, I am sure," said the lady. "We must trust and pray. I would let you be in charge of her today, but I feel sure Big Mo will not leave the hospital without her. If he should, I will let you know. I will go now and sleep for a few hours, but if you need me I will come." She squeezed Resa's hand and left the room.

For several minutes Resa stood beside the bed crying softly. Then she slipped out of the room and motioned for the nurse, Neda, to take over. Mo would soon finish his breakfast and return to the sleeping child.

Dookie Wakes Up

AS BIG Mo entered the room, Neda smiled and whispered, "She is still asleep, but I think she will be waking soon. The fever is gone, and the swelling seems to be going down fast. She is a pretty child."

Big Mo stood looking at the little girl. "To me she is beautiful; she is everything. How thankful I am that I brought her here in time!"

Dookie opened her eyes and looked into the man's face. "Big Mo!" she said, reaching up her little hands to clasp him around his neck.

"My precious one!" he said, gathering her in his arms and holding her close. Then he laid her gently back on the white bed.

"Where are we?" Dookie asked, looking around at the unfamiliar surroundings. "When did we come here?"

"Big Mo!" she said, reaching up her little hands to clasp him around his neck. "My precious one!" he said, gathering her in his arms.

"This is the doctor's room," he told her.

"I don't want to be here," she said, clinging to Mo in fear.

"But this is not the charm doctor's place, Dookie, this is the Christian mission. Don't you remember the long white buildings with red-tiled roofs?"

"Yes," said Dookie, looking around.

Then Mo told her how the doctor had taken care of the snake bite on her leg, and how he had used the magic needle with the magic water for snake bites.

"But the mission doctor," objected Dookie; "did he cast a spell on me? You told me that Christians were the most dangerous of all people."

"I have been greatly mistaken. I know now that the God in heaven is more powerful than the charm doctor and the spirits and devil gods."

"The mission hospital," said the girl, looking with wonder at the glass cases of bottles and instruments.

"Did we come up the long, winding road like the one we took the day we followed the bees?" asked Dookie.

"Yes, my little one," said Mo.

"Who is that?" she whispered, looking at Neda.

"She is one of the kind nurses," said Mo. "She takes care of you and the other patients in the hospital."

"What are all those bottles for?" questioned the girl.

"I cannot tell you," said Mo. "But I am sure the doctor knows. He has wonderful magic for snake bites. See, the swelling is almost gone. The magic is working. I am so glad I brought you here."

Neda paused in the doorway. "I am glad that you came from breakfast in time to be with her when she woke up. I would have had a hard time explaining things to her."

During a break in the morning activities at the hospital, Big Mo talked to the kind doctor, and talked about paying the bill.

"When the rice harvest is over," he concluded, "I will sell my cows and everything, and build a little house close to the mission so she can attend school when it starts again. I want her to learn about the God in heaven, and what He can do for us. But before I leave the village, there is something I am going to do." Mo clenched his fists tightly as if in great determination.

"What is that, my friend?" the doctor questioned.

"I am going to investigate this wicked burning of innocent babies at funerals. I have long felt that it was wrong, but I was powerless to do anything about it. I feared what the spirits might do to me. Now I know there is a God in heaven who can help me. With these two hands I took one little bundle from the burning flames, but it was too late." Mo showed the doctor the scars on his hands. "But I am no longer afraid of the charm doctor or the spirits. I will go to the headman of the village; I will go to court."

"You may count on me to help," said the doctor. "I will be glad to help you in any way I can to rid the Savaras of this terrible curse. You are undertaking a great task, but I am sure that the God in heaven will help you in time of need."

When Dookie was ready to go home, Big Mo carried her from the mission hospital, down the stone walk to the winding road. From the window Resa watched them go. The mission lady stood beside her.

"I could not take the girl from him," said Resa. "She loves him, and he can do so much for her. I will never let him know that I saw her. She is better off with him. He makes a good father for her; he is so strong." Resa wept softly. "I wonder if I will see her again."

"Yes, I'm sure you will see her," said the lady. "There are plans for her to come to the mission school at the next session, and he will build a home close to the mission. For her sake and his, let it be this way so that they may learn to become Christians. It has all worked out for their good. The loving Father has let you see your daughter again after all you suffered."

"Yes," said Resa softly. "Dookie means grief; but the Lord has changed the grief to joy. I am glad that I could see her again."

Big Mo gathered the charm doctor in his strong arms, and threw him into the pond. The man waved his arms and legs in wild commotion.

At the Spring

OWN the long, winding road toward the village went Big Mo, carrying Dookie. He sang as he went, making up cheerful songs as they went along. They were songs about trees, rice fields, singing birds, water buffaloes, and little girls.

Dookie patted his cheek lovingly and said, "You sing better songs than you ever did before. I like your songs. Please sing one about Spindlelegs and the lotus pool where she drinks. I think that would be a lovely song."

Big Mo sang for the joy in his heart. When he sang about Spindlelegs, he suddenly remembered the cows that he had neglected. He hoped the woodcutter had done the chores for him. The man had a kind face and he had told him the truth about the wonderful magic for snake bites. No doubt the woodcutter could use the money he received from the sale of the milk.

As they neared the village street where the markets were located, Mo stopped singing. He held his head high and had a friendly smile for everyone he met. The world seemed so different now that he understood many things. Fear no longer clutched at his heart; the spirits would not take his little girl from him. The God in heaven was stronger and more powerful than the charm doctor and all the spirits and devil gods. Mo wanted to learn more about the true God. Little Dookie would go to the mission school to learn about Him.

"Shall we stop at the spring for a cool drink?" suggested Mo. "This time, Dookie, you will sit on some big leaves on the bank while I swim. We wouldn't want to get that clean bandage wet, would we?"

"Of course not," said Dookie.

Big Mo made her comfortable by the pond, and then he plunged in for a swim; he did not stay in the water very long, for he wanted to get home and see about his cows. Suddenly he heard Dookie scream. There, right behind her, with his long, bony fingers around her neck, was the charm doctor!

Big Mo made a great leap and his big hands loosened the hold on Dookie. He threw the little man down on the sand.

102

"What were you doing to her?" demanded Big Mo, standing over him. "If you ever touch her again, I'll shake you to pieces."

"I was only going to take her," began the charm doctor in his high-pitched voice. He hesitated, for he was afraid of the big man of the village standing so tall above him.

"Take her where? To the shrine? To the temple? Where?"

But the evil man was too frightened to answer. Big Mo leaned over, gathered the charm doctor in his strong arms and threw him into the pond. With a gurgling scream the man struggled and sputtered, waving his arms and legs in wild commotion, trying to get out. Evidently he was not accustomed to water, for it seemed to be a great irritation to him. Big Mo stepped into the pond, and every time the man tried to get up, Mo pushed him down again.

"The curse of the spirits be on you," the charm doctor gurgled and screamed. How angry he was! "The curse of the demons, the curse of the snakes!" Dookie put her hands over her ears. She did not like to hear the terrible words.

Finally Big Mo pulled the trembling man out of the pond, shook him, and then gave him a shove toward the path. "Now go, and stay away from my little girl from this time on," he said. "I do not fear the spirits or what they can do. I am no longer afraid of you or your charms and curses. And if I ever hear of your putting tiny babies on the funeral pyre again, I will put you on it. Remember, I can take it to court. The mission doctor said he would help me. Let me tell you there is a power even stronger than the magic of the mission doctor, and that is the power of the great God in heaven. He made the sun and the moon and the stars and the rain. You had better think a long time before you defy Him by scaring people with your charms and curses, and by putting tiny babies on spirit shrines and funeral pyres. Now, get out of my sight."

Gathering up his dripping garment, the charm doctor lost no time in disappearing. Big Mo picked up Dookie and carried her up the path to the mud house with the thatched roof.

"Rest on the mat, little one," said Mo. "I will see what we can find for supper. It looks like the woodcutter has been a good housekeeper while we were gone. The milk jars are clean, the rice kettle has been emptied and scrubbed, and everything is in its proper place."

"It's good to be home again," said Dookie, taking her wooden doll in her arms. "It was nice at the mission, though, and the mission lady and Neda were good to me."

"Yes," said Mo, as he poured water into the rice kettle. "Just the two of us here at home; but Kola will soon be coming with the cows."

The Woodcutter's Story

WHEN the rice was ready to eat, Big Mo spread the usual big leaves on the mat, dipped some of the hot rice with his bare hands onto the leaves, and sat down to eat with Dookie. Did Mo forget to put on the silverware? No, it was the custom to eat rice and curry with the fingers.

Playfully Dookie fed little bites of rice to her doll. This was the one Mo had carved when she was a tiny girl, and it was still her favorite toy. She laughed as Mo made wry faces.

"Dolly says that bite is too hot," said Big Mo teasingly. "Dolly says that bite is too salty. Dolly says that bite is too sour."

Dookie laughed and laughed. Big Mo was so much fun! He played with her as if he were a a little girl, too.

Then Dookie said, "I think I hear Kola coming."

Mo looked out of the open doorway. "Yes, Kola is coming with the cows, and he has the kind woodcutter with him. He took care of the cows while we were gone. He is the one who told me about the wonderful magic of the mission doctor."

"Good evening!" The greetings were friendly and sincere. The woodcutter was glad to see that Dookie was able to be home again, and Kola stopped to talk a few minutes after putting the cows in the enclosure.

The woodcutter offered to milk the cows while Big Mo finished his supper, but Mo said, "You have already done more for me than I can ever repay. But come, sit down and have supper with us. There is plenty of rice and you are welcome to eat with us."

"Thank you," said the woodcutter, taking a leaf from the stand and squatting before the rice kettle. For a brief moment he bowed his head in an attitude of prayer, then he reached his hand into the kettle and took some rice, and began to eat.

"I have many things to tell you," said Mo. He recounted his experience from the time the woodcutter advised him to take Dookie to the mission. He concluded with the story of the charm doctor's surprise visit at the pond, and of the charm doctor's sudden ducking.

"Perhaps I should not have been so rough with him," said Mo; "but I will teach him to keep his hands off the little one." He rose, took down the milk jars, and got ready to milk the cows.

"If you will bring the jars," he told the woodcutter, "I will take Dookie." They went to the enclosure where the cows were waiting.

When the milking was done and the milk had been strained and put in the jars to cool, Big Mo, the woodcutter, and Dookie sat on the stones outside the door of the house and talked while they watched the moon rise over the palm trees.

"I, too, have a story to tell you," began the woodcutter. Mo was so glad to have someone to talk to, to eat with, and to confide in, that he was guilty of forgetting his duty as a host.

"I am sorry, my friend, that I have been doing most of the talking tonight," said Mo. "I fear I have been almost rude. Please forgive me, and we will gladly listen to your story."

"It happened before I became a Christian," said the woodcutter. "I did not know about the God in heaven; but, like so many people in the Savara villages, I was in constant fear of the spirits and the curses of the charm doctor. At the time of the great drought, my rice crop dried up. I was a poor man with only one cow, and I depended upon the sale of milk to support my wife and me. I know now that it was dishonest to put water in the milk that I sold, but I was desperate at the time. I will confess that often the

107

water was not even clean. When the calf came, I was happy, but within the week a spotted leopard came and took the calf from me. It did no good to seek the advice of the charm doctor, for he only told me it was the will of the spirits. They were angry with me, he said, because I did not pay a large sum of money to the charm doctor. I was so poor I could hardly afford to put flowers on the shrine. Then, to avoid greater misfortune, the charm doctor took my one cow, to prevent further evil by the spirits.

"My wife became ill from lack of proper food. I scuttled around the garbage heaps like the mangy, skinny cats that ate the same fare. When our baby was born, my wife was so weak and ill that she died that same night. It seemed I had lost everything but the baby. She was so tiny and helpless; she cried pitifully all the time. The charm doctor told me that the reason all the trouble had come to me was because the baby was a girl. He said that to appease the spirits I must place my newborn baby girl on the funeral pyre of my dear wife that morning. A kind neighbor prepared the little shroud to wrap her in.

"At the funeral I felt I could not endure the sorrow. Everything I had was gone. There lay my wife with my infant daughter, still alive, resting on her bosom, ready to be burned. I had to do something! While the charm doctor was busy lighting the fire on the one side of the pile of the dry twigs, I slipped around and snatched

108

the little one and ran out into the jungle. I ran like a wild animal. How far I ran, I do not know. But when I was too exhausted to run any farther, I dug a hole in the ground like an animal, and crawled in with my baby to hide. I gave the little one a name—Doorbhagini, which means 'bad luck.' I did everything I could to keep her alive. I fed her the juice of berries. I chewed grass and gave her the liquid from it. I secretly milked a neighbor's goat in order to give her milk. Then one day I found that little Doorbhagini had a sore mouth, so in utter despair I took her to the mission lady in a nearby village. She did her best to save the baby, but it was too late. The Christians at the mission were kind to me; they told me of the God in heaven who loved me. They had a very different funeral for my little Doorbhagini, and soon I became a Christian. Since then I have been cutting wood and earning an honest living wherever I can."

The woodcutter's story was ended. Little Dookie had been listening with interest, and there were tears in her eyes. "Poor little Doorbhagini," she said. "I am sorry you lost your little girl. I would have loved her, too."

"Thank you," said the woodcutter. "If she had lived she would be about your size, and ready for school."

"I think I will go to the mission school when the next term starts," said Dookie. "My friend Luani goes to the school."

8—D.S.M.

Big Mo thought he should do a bit of explaining. "It would be too far to go to the mission school from here, so I plan to buy some land and build a bigger house nearer to the mission. Would you be interested in this place, my friend, with three good cows in the bargain?"

"Me? This place?" echoed the woodcutter.

"Yes," said Mo. "And there are good rice terraces on the hillside to the north."

"But I am a poor woodcutter. I have no money, and this place would cost many rupees. I could never pay you."

"I am your brother now, for I, too, am a Christian," said Mo. "I will make it easy for you because you told me where to go in my great need. Because of you I still have my little girl. We can see the headman of the village in the morning and sign the papers. You are my brother; I will trust you."

"But the cows?" asked the woodcutter.

"I will need only one. I will give the other to my friend Kola."

"Big Mo," said Dookie, "can we keep Spindlelegs?"

"We will keep Spindlelegs. Someday soon she will have a calf, and then, perhaps, I will be a 'two-cow' man again."

"Thank you, my Christian brother. You will make me rich indeed. But now I must go, for we all need rest. May the God in heaven watch over us all and protect us through the night."

110

After the woodcutter had gone, Mo spread the two sleeping mats on the floor. He put the rice kettle back on the flat stones of the fireplace, then took the broad leaves and threw them over the fence to the cows. Soon the man and his little girl were sound asleep.

The Little Bundle

ONE morning before the sun was up, Kola came running up the hill path and shook the bamboo gate vigorously, calling, "Mo, Big Mo."

Startled out of a sound sleep, Mo arose hastily, put on his outer garment, and asked, "Are you all right, Kola? Why are you here so early?"

Quite out of breath, Kola tried to explain. "They are getting ready for a funeral. A young mother died, but the baby still lives. The charm doctor brags that you do not dare show your face at the burning. He is planning a trick."

"Sit down, Kola. Get your breath and then tell me more. You are a good friend to come and tell me."

Kola told Mo what he had heard in the village.

The charm doctor had dared Mo to come. Something within the big man accepted the challenge. All the pent-up feelings of fight came back to him. He would be there. This would be no ordinary fight, for it was the chance he had long been awaiting. The mission doctor would stand with him, and they could take the matter to the court.

"Of course I am going!" said Big Mo.

"But little Dookie?" questioned Kola. "You wouldn't leave her here alone."

"Oh, no," said Mo. "I wouldn't leave her here. It might be a trick, so I will take her with me. If trouble comes you can watch her. I trust her with you, Kola. On our way I will ask the woodcutter to care for the cows. We may be late coming home."

Soon Dookie, Kola, and Mo were on their way to the village. It was daylight when they reached the main street, and the people were milling about because of the funeral ceremony.

"We will go out by the river and hide in the bushes beyond the pile of wood," said Mo. "I wish that Dookie did not have to see this, but we cannot leave her anywhere. I do not know what trick the charm doctor will try next. He is so angry at me."

When they reached the hiding place beyond the funeral pyre, they crouched low and waited. Mo fed Dookie some of the rice in the gourd, hoping she would go back to sleep. But the girl was not sleepy. The early hour, the hasty trip to the

113

village, and the mystery of it all, made her brown eyes wide with wonder and questioning.

"You must do exactly as I tell you, my precious one," said Mo. "Do not be afraid. We know that these ceremonies are wrong, and that the God in heaven is not pleased. Somehow I feel in my heart that He will help us."

"I will do as you say," said Dookie, nestling her head against his shoulder. "I am not afraid with you here."

"But I may not be right here beside you all the time."

"I will not be afraid with Kola."

"Here they come!" said Kola, as he peered around the bushes and the pile of wood. "The charm doctor is leading the way, and there are several villagers coming across the grasslands. What will he do if he finds us here?"

"We will wait and not be afraid."

"But are you sure that the God in heaven is stronger than the spirits and the charm doctor?"

"I am sure," said Big Mo confidently. "Did I not tell you that He saved my little girl?"

Down behind the bushes they watched as preparations were made for the ceremony. The larger bundle was placed on the logs and the dry grass and twigs. Then the smaller bundle was laid on top.

By this time there was a crowd of villagers standing around. They had come from every direction, some out of curiosity, but others to

114

cry and moan in the usual manner at funerals.

The husband of the deceased was there with a small group of relatives. They were watching the charm doctor as he began his ceremonial dance. The husband seemed unconcerned that this was a sorrowful occasion, for he took a drink from a gourd that hung by a string around his neck and joined in the weird chant of the mourners.

Big Mo did not like the attitude of the father. How could he be so unconcerned when his little baby was lying in a shroud, waiting helplessly to be burned alive by the spirit-fearing Savaras?

Mo set his teeth and clenched his fists. Then he gave instructions to Kola: "That grass is very dry; it will burn quickly. I will have to work fast. When the fire has been set the charm doctor will turn to the people. At that moment I will rush out, take the little bundle, and run back with it. I will give it to you while I carry Dookie. We will run and hide in the clump of bamboo until the crowd leaves. Then we will go around behind the spirit tree to the woodcutter's home and be safe. Do you understand, Kola?"

Kola nodded. He still feared the spirits and the charm doctor, yet he believed that Big Mo was doing the right thing in saving the baby.

They were close enough to the pyre to see the movement of the little bundle. Kola thought he heard a tiny cry, but he could not be sure. So many people were moaning and children were screaming.

115

Big Mo heard the cry and he saw the movements of hands and feet within the shroud. His nerves were tense. He crouched, waiting for the moment. Then he ran! But before he reached the pile of burning grass and twigs, he was stopped. Someone grabbed him from behind, and his arms were fastened in a tight wrestling hold. He looked back to see who had hindered his plan. It was Big Thau, the challenger!

The Wrath of the Charm Doctor

"LET me go!" cried Mo, struggling frantically to be free. But Big Thau only squeezed the harder and gloated in his ear, "I told you I would get you someday, and this time the charm doctor pays me!"

"Let me go, you coward," shouted Mo. "I won over you fair and square; but you come at me from behind. Are you too much of a coward to face me?" Mo twisted and turned, trying to break the hold; but even with his great strength he was powerless, held in the viselike grip of the man hired by the charm doctor.

Dancing around and around on his sandaled feet, waving his fire stick wildly in the air, the little charm doctor gloated over the fact that at last he had Big Mo in his power. He laughed and

Dancing around on his sandaled feet, and waving his fire stick wildly,
the charm doctor gloated that at last he had Big Mo in his power.

boasted in his high-pitched voice, "Now I have you where I want you. You can't get away from me this time. You dared to duck me in the pond. You treated me like a dog. Now I call all the spirits to put a curse on you. They will teach you not to interfere with my business. Big man, indeed!" He waved his fire stick threateningly in Mo's face.

Suddenly the wind began to blow, causing the flames on the funeral pyre to blaze higher. Soon they would envelop the whole pile, even the little bundle. The father stood back, drinking liquor from his gourd, making no effort to save his child. Mo struggled and twisted, trying in vain to break the hold. The excited crowd screamed louder. They did not know what was taking place, but they were excited. Above the roar of the screaming and moaning, above the crackling of the flames and the whistling of the wind, Big Mo shouted to the charm doctor, "I no longer fear you or the spirits. The God in heaven is stronger than all. I believe in Him, and I call upon Him now to put a stop to this terrible practice. If it is His will, He will save that tiny newborn baby from the fire. I tried to save it, but you hired this coward to sneak up behind me. Neither one of you dared to face me. Now in my weakness I call upon the great God in heaven to save that baby from the flames!"

"Is the tiny baby afraid?" asked Dookie. "Is that why it is crying?"
"I think it is hungry. It has not been fed for a long time," said Mo.

Help From the Thunder

BIG Mo lifted his face to heaven. Somewhere up there, beyond the dark clouds, was the God of the universe, the Creator of all things. The man prayed, "I can do nothing myself with Big Thau holding my arms. I ask You, the God who saved my precious one from the snake bite, to save the tiny one from the flames. Amen."

It was Mo's first prayer, and he was very earnest. He had done his best, but now he was helpless. He could hear the fire crackling, and he felt the wind blowing dust and smoke in his face. He looked at the fire, and saw that the flames had not yet reached the little bundle! The wind was blowing the fire in the other direction!

Suddenly the people were startled by a loud clap of thunder. Drops of rain fell from the dark clouds overhead. With a lump in his throat, Mo remembered little Dookie. How frightened she always was when she heard the big thunder! Was she frightened now without him to comfort her? However, she was safe with Kola, hidden under the big leaves of the bushes.

Faster and faster came the rain, driven by the wind. This was unexpected, for it was not the rainy season. The people began to scatter, running for shelter. Mothers wrapped their saris around their children and hurried away.

Big Mo suddenly realized that the God in heaven had sent this sudden storm, even in the dry season, as an answer to his prayer!

The charm doctor still danced around, waving his fire stick, muttering threats, and calling on the spirits to stop the rain. Big Thau loosened his hold, hit Mo a blow in the middle of his back, and ran for shelter.

With his hands free at last, Mo ran to the smoldering pyre, snatched up the wet bundle, and hurried behind the bushes where Kola and Dookie were anxiously waiting. Mo felt the tiny body move in his hands. The baby was alive! The wind had kept the smoke and flames back, and then the rain had quenched the fire.

Mo tore open the little shroud. "Oh," said Dookie, "it is a real baby!"

"What will you do with it?" asked Kola.

"I will take it to the mission. They will know what to do with it. The doctor will take it to the headman, and the court will do something with the father and the charm doctor. The mission doctor told me they can put the father in jail and that this action might stop the evil practice. Kola, do you understand now? Surely you can see that the great God in heaven is more powerful than the charm doctor."

"Yes, Mo, I believe. I am no longer afraid of the charm doctor or the spirits. But that thunder really sounds loud sometimes!"

"We were afraid," said Dookie. "We both wished you would hurry and come."

The rain continued, and the rescuers stayed under the protection of the big leaves. Little Dookie snuggled against Big Mo every time the thunder rumbled. Although Kola said he wasn't afraid, he didn't like the storm. The tiny baby cried, but Big Mo patted it tenderly.

"Are you afraid, too, Big Mo?" asked Dookie. "You are shivering."

"No, my precious one, I am no longer afraid. I know now who makes the rain. He sends it to us when we need it. I will always believe and trust the God in heaven." He bowed his head and said, "Thank You, God, for saving the tiny baby from the fire."

"Is the tiny baby afraid?" asked Dookie, touching the wet covering lightly with her hand. "Is that why it is crying?"

"I think it is hungry. It has not been fed for a long time," said Mo.

"May I hold it, just for a minute? Maybe, since I am a girl, it will think I am its mother."

Big Mo placed the bundle in the girl's arm. "There you are, little play mother," he said. "Hold it carefully."

Dookie had never held a baby before. It was warm and soft, not hard and stiff like the wooden dolls Mo had carved for her. For a few moments the baby responded to the gentle touch, but then it started to cry again.

"Here, Big Mo, you take it. I think you are a better mother."

"The storm is over," said Mo, looking out from under the broad leaves. "The clouds are breaking and the blue is showing in the sky above us. We will go at once to the mission. The lady will know what to do for this tiny one. Will you come with me, Kola?"

"I will go with you as far as the market," said Kola. "Then I will get the cows and take them to the grasslands. The woodcutter will have finished milking, and they will want to eat. I will tell the woodcutter to care for the milk. Will you be gone long?"

"I cannot tell how long, Kola. It is far to the mission, and we may be late getting home. You are my good friend; I will give you many annas for your work."

At the Mission

AFTER parting with Kola at the market place, Big Mo and Dookie went through the puddles in the winding road that led to the mission. The sun came out, and everything became hot and steamy.

"I am tired, Big Mo," said Dookie with a sigh.

"Of course you are. I should have thought of that." He lifted her up so she could ride on his hip while he held her with one arm.

After the doctor had given the baby into the care of the mission lady, he listened carefully to Mo's story.

"We will make this a test case," said the doctor. "We will bring both the father and the charm doctor before the court. I am sure this will help to stop the evil practice. Now, as to the

125

infant. Are there relatives who would care for her? The grandmother? The father? Surely there is someone who would take her and raise her. Like Dookie, she needs much love and security."

"I do not know any relatives who would be interested," said Mo. "They made a pretense of mourning, but no one lifted a hand to save the baby, not even the father!"

"When I mentioned someone who would take her and raise her, I really was not thinking of relatives." The doctor winked through his glasses at Dookie, who was sitting on the couch beside Mo. "I hardly think they deserve a nice baby after what they tried to do to her, do you, Dookie?"

"No," said the girl. There was a sweet seriousness in the little face. "I think she should have a nice daddy like Big Mo."

Soon the mission lady brought in the baby. It had been bathed, fed, and wrapped in a blanket. The lady placed the sleeping infant in Mo's arms. Suddenly the idea broke through to Big Mo. The doctor was referring to him! He looked down at the tiny bit of helpless humanity, and compassion came over him. Mo looked at the doctor questioningly. "Do you mean me? Do you think I could—"

"Can you think of anyone who would be more concerned or more fitted to care for this little one than you are after you saved her from a ter-

Suddenly the idea broke through to Big Mo. The doctor was referring to him! He looked down at the tiny baby, and compassion came over him.

rible death? I think it is time for Dookie to have a sister. What do you say, young lady?"

"Oh, yes," she agreed, clapping her hands. "I could help take care of the baby. I could be her play mother."

Big Mo put his arm around Dookie and held her close. "Whatever you say, my precious one. Do you think we can manage?"

Dookie put her arms around Mo's neck. "Oh, I'd love it," she said earnestly.

"I think it is going to work out all right," said the doctor. "I'll have some papers made out at the court that will give you rights to the baby. Then no one can take her from you. Now, will you be our guests at the dining hall? It is time for dinner."

"I was getting hungry," said Dookie, as she took the hand of the mission lady and followed Big Mo and the doctor.

The Three of Us

WHEN Big Mo, Dookie, and the baby left the hospital, the little girl carried a package the mission lady had given them to make it easier to care for the baby. It was a long walk to the village, and up the hill path to the house. Part of the time Mo carried Dookie on his back, with her arms clasped around his neck. He carried the baby on one arm and the package in the other. When they went in the house, they found that the cows had been milked and the jars of milk were cooling in the water tank. The strainer was washed and hung up to dry.

"There are no chores to do tonight," said Mo. "All we need to do is to eat supper and go to bed."

"There will be a big moon tonight," said Dookie. "The two of us can sit on the step and talk about the God in heaven."

"Aren't you tired and sleepy, my precious? This has been a long day, and we were up so very early."

"What you say is right," said Dookie obediently, looking at the sleeping baby on the mat.

Big Mo soon had supper ready, and the two ate in silence. Mo noticed how quiet and reserved the girl was. It had been such a long, trying day for her, but a good night's rest would work wonders.

Suddenly the words came to his mind, "the two of us." Could it be that Dookie thought that this tiny baby would take her place in his affections? He had fed the baby first and placed it on Dookie's mat! There she sat with a downcast face. He would not hurt his little girl even if it meant giving the baby to someone else to raise. He arose from supper and gathered Dookie up in his arms. "My precious one," he said, "we will sit on the stone step, just the two of us, and watch the moon rise."

They watched the moon rise. They talked of the love of God, the wonderful Creator of all things. Mo did not mention the baby, for he did not want the girl to feel it was taking her place.

"Big Mo, don't you love the tiny one even a little bit?" asked Dookie. "You don't even talk about her. Will you love her, too, and hold her tight like you do me? I think she would like to be loved, for she doesn't have any mother but you!"

130

"If you want me to, I will. But no one will ever take your place in my heart. I'll try to love her, too, if you want me to."

"I'm glad," said Dookie. "Do you think she will ever be as big as I am? She is so little and helpless now."

Mo realized there were no jealous feelings in the girl. She was sweet and unselfish.

"What are we going to call her?" asked Dookie. "We can't call her the tiny one. She might grow up to be bigger than I am."

"Of course she must have a name," said Mo. "I should have thought of it before. We will not choose an ugly one for her, because we are no longer afraid that the spirits will take her from us."

"It should be a happy name," said Dookie, "because we are happy to have her."

"Suppose we call her Sookie, which means 'joy,' " suggested the man.

Dookie clapped her hands. "I like that." She jumped up and said, "Come on, Big Mo, let's get little Sookie, so all three of us can sit here together. Then we can tell the God in heaven how happy we are to be a part of His big family."

"All right, little play mother," returned Big Mo.

Moving Day

THE days were busy for Big Mo, as well as for the woodcutter and some of the boys from the school. They helped to build the new house not far from the mission. Luani's mother kept Dookie and Sookie at her house during the hours Big Mo was working.

"I just can't wait!" said Dookie to Luani, as she rocked little Sookie in her arms. "Tomorrow morning we will go to live in our new house by the three hills."

"I will miss you," said Luani. "We have had good times together. Sookie is so tiny and cuddly. I love her."

"I love her, too," said Dookie, patting the baby gently. "And when I think of how we got her, I love her so much more. It is your turn to

132

hold her now, Luani. You are a good play mother."

Luani carefully took the tiny baby in her arms, holding the little body close to her own. "Thank you, Dookie, for sharing her with me. I wish I had a baby sister."

The two girls thought of school days ahead, and Luani said, "I know you'll like school. We make marks with the magic stick and the marks talk to us. They tell us many things. But what I like best of all is when the mission lady sings to us. I feel so happy I almost cry."

"It must be wonderful," said Dookie softly.

Very early the next morning Big Mo hurried about to have everything ready when the mission boys came with the oxcart. He built the fire in the corner, put fresh water in the kettle for the rice, and then went to milk Spindlelegs. Mo was thankful that he no longer feared the charm doctor or Sookie's father, for he trusted the God of heaven, who showed His love in a wonderful way. Mo looked at the rosy gleam of dawn beyond the palm trees and said a prayer of thanks to the One who made the sun, the rain, and the whole universe.

"I will use these hands to work for You," he said reverently. "I will no longer use them to fight. Help me to care for my two precious ones, that they may learn to go in the way that is best. Bless me in my new work at the mission."

When the morning chores were finished,

133

Sookie started to cry for her breakfast. Dookie held the baby in her arms and rocked her to and fro, singing softly.

"I'll get her breakfast right away," said Big Mo.

"Is it today, Big Mo?" asked Dookie, when the little one was busy drinking from her bottle.

"Yes, my precious, this is the day we move. The boys from the mission will be coming up the hill path with the oxcart."

"I am so happy," said Dookie. Then she put her head down close to Sookie and began to cry. Big Mo could not understand this action, and he bent down and asked, "Why the tears, my precious one? Don't you want to move to our new home? It will be so much nicer than this one. Dry those tears and tell me why you are crying if you are so happy."

Dookie could not quite explain. This must be what Luani meant when she said she was so happy that she had to cry.

"Will it have a doorstep where we can sit in the evening and watch the moon come up?" asked the girl.

"Yes," said Mo.

"Will the step be big enough for three of us to sit side by side?"

"Yes," answered Mo. "And we will see the same river, and the same moon. There are palm trees to see just like the ones here. I hope you will like the new home."

Mo realized that this was the only home Dookie had known, and it might take some time to make adjustments.

"Will God be there, too?" asked Dookie.

"Yes, my little one, God will be there. We will be living near the mission, where the kind doctor and the mission lady have their home."

For several minutes Mo talked about the new house and the surprise that was awaiting the girl. Taking a corner of Sookie's blanket, Mo wiped away the girl's tears and placed a tender kiss on her forehead.

"You didn't kiss little Sookie," said Dookie shyly, as Mo went to the corner to stir the rice in the kettle. Mo came back, bent down, and placed a kiss on the brown cheek of the tiny one.

"There, little play mother," he said. "I will try not to forget again. You see, she was so busy with her bottle she didn't seem to care."

After breakfast, Dookie gathered up her few treasures. She carefully placed in a basket the wooden dolls and animals that Mo had carved for her. She folded up her sleeping blanket, then made a packet of the baby's things and placed them on top of the blanket.

"I think I hear the oxcart," she said. When she looked out the door she called, "It's coming! It's coming!"

With the help of Tim and Orlo, the oxcart was soon loaded with the few articles that Mo and Dookie were to take with them. There were cooking pots, axes, hoes, milk jars, blankets, sleeping mats, honey jars, a bottle of oil, a small bench, Dookie's box, and the baby's packet.

"I guess that is all," said Big Mo, looking about the empty room. In one corner was the wooden peg where the tsu gourd had formerly hung. Mo smiled. He had no further use for tsu, since he was a Christian.

The boys tied Spindlelegs to the back of the cart, and the cow's young calf jumped here and there, kicking up her feet.

"You won't feel so frisky at the end of the trip," said Mo.

"Frisky!" said Dookie. "Let's call the new calf 'Frisky.' I think that is the right name for her."

"It will be as you say," said Mo. "But it is a long way to the mission, and I doubt if she will live up to her name by that time."

Dookie and the boys laughed as the calf capered around.

"She knows we are talking about her," said Tim. "She is showing off for us."

Mo lifted Dookie into the cart, and she sat on the bench and held the sleeping Sookie on her lap. After the boys had tightened the ropes that fastened the canopy over the cart, Tim climbed in and Orlo started the oxen on their way. When he was sure that the calf would follow its mother, Mo climbed on the cart, and it lumbered down the stony path toward the village.

Dookie swayed from side to side as the cart wheels bumped along. Mo watched her turn to look at the little mud hut with the thatched roof that had been her only home. He wondered if she would be homesick in the new place. He hoped she would be pleased with the surprise that was waiting for her!

When they reached the village road, the bumps were less frequent. The boys halted the cart in the shade of a big tree beside the road. The oxen rested and were given a drink of water from the spring.

When the sun was high overhead the boys stopped again by a lotus pond. While the oxen and Spindlelegs ate the green grass, Big Mo shared the remaining rice in the kettle with Dookie and the two boys. Sookie had another bottle of diluted cow's milk sweetened with honey. Soon they were back on the road, jogging slowly along.

As Dookie listened to the "click click" of the oxen's hoofs on the hard road and the "creak creak" of the cart wheels, she became sleepy. Mo arranged the bench and the sleeping mats so that Dookie and Sookie could both lie down and rest. When the oxcart stopped, Dookie woke up.

"We're here!" announced Big Mo, jumping down from the cart.

Dookie sat up and looked around. To the north she could see the mission buildings. To the east she glimpsed the shining river and the tall palm trees. To the south was the jungle that seemed to climb up the sides of the three hills. There, nestled among some scattered trees and bushes, she saw the stone house that was to be her new home.

"Oh!" said Dookie, pushing her hair back from her eyes. "I didn't think it would be this nice!" After Big Mo had helped her down from the cart, the girl ran to the door, and Mo followed with Sookie in his arms.

Dookie noticed the wide cement step, the screen door, the red-tiled roof, and the screened windows. She opened the door and went inside, stepping lightly on the bright tile floor. As she looked about, she noticed another door leading into a smaller room.

"This is your surprise," said Mo. "A surprise for you and little Sookie."

"A room for Sookie and me!" Dookie put her arms around Mo. "This is the best surprise!"

"Now you be play mother and hold Sookie while I bring in the sleeping mats; then we will take Spindlelegs and Frisky to their new home behind the house."

In a few minutes the oxcart was unloaded, and Mo paid the boys generously.

"Big Mo," said the girl, "I know we will be happy here. I am glad for the screens. They will keep out leopards, tigers, bears, and big snakes."

"Yes," agreed Mo. "And the angels of God will keep away evil spirits that might harm us."

138

Figures That Talk

ON THAT wonderful first day of school, Dookie was up before sunrise. She scrubbed and scrubbed her face and hands, smoothed down her hair, and arranged her new sari that was just for school.

Mo was doing the morning chores when Dookie came around the corner of the house. "See! Do I look good enough to go to school?" asked the girl.

"Just like a little princess!" said Mo. "But aren't you early?"

"I couldn't wait," explained Dookie. "I can't sleep when I am so happy."

"I can see the sparkle of your eyes," said Mo. "I'll be in to get breakfast soon."

"I am hungry, too!"

But Dookie was so excited that she could hardly eat her rice. When she heard the drums at the mission, her eyes were wide in eagerness. Mo picked up the small packet and the sleeping Sookie.

The mission lady welcomed them with a smile at the door of the schoolroom. She held out her hands for the tiny one, and Mo placed Sookie in her arms. "One of the Indian nurses has offered to care for the baby during school hours," said the mission lady. "In that way, Dookie will be free to do her classwork. I think it will be a favor to let the nurse care for Sookie, for she lost her own baby when it was tiny. She will be very tender and devoted."

Mo went to get his instructions for work from the mission doctor. He paused to look back and wave at Dookie as she joined Luani and the other children entering the schoolroom.

When the drums beat again, Luani led Dookie by the hand to one of the small benches. "We will sit here for the first part," explained Luani. "After we sing and pray and have our story, we will sit at those tables and make magic figures that talk."

Dookie listened attentively to the mission lady as she told the story. Suddenly she realized that the lady was no longer holding the baby.

"Where is Sookie? Is she all right?" asked the girl. "Are you sure that the lady is a good play mother?"

140

The mission lady paused in the story to reassure Dookie that the baby could not be in better hands. "Before we go to class, I will take you to see her." She patted Dookie gently on the arm.

"It is as you say," said Dookie meekly.

But Dookie was worried, for everything was new and strange. What if Sookie cried? What if the play mother was cross? Where was Mo? What was he doing? She knew he was working, but he seemed so far away! Suddenly big tears came into her eyes.

The mission lady was singing a song about Jesus. Luani leaned over and whispered, "I told you when she sings it makes you so happy you feel like crying."

But that was not why Dookie was crying. She couldn't explain it, even to herself.

After the songs and prayer there was a short recess. The boys and girls went outside to play until the drums beat. At this time the mission lady took Dookie to the room where the laundry was folded and put on the shelves. "Here she is," said the mission lady. "See! The tiny one is fast asleep in the laundry basket. Doesn't she look peaceful and sweet? Do you suppose she is having pleasant dreams?"

Dookie glanced at Sookie and then at the lady who was folding towels at a long table.

"Is she the play mother?" whispered Dookie.

"Yes," said the mission lady.

"She doesn't look like a cross mother."

141

"Oh, no," said the mission lady. "Resa is sweet and kind. She will be good to little Sookie."

"I had a mother once," said Dookie. "Her name was Resa, too. Big Mo told me about her. She was not a cross mother. I think she was kind and sweet."

"I am sure she was," agreed the mission lady. Then she said, "Resa, come and meet Dookie, the baby's sister. She was a bit anxious to see that you are a good play mother."

Resa stood looking at the child before her. How she longed to take her in her arms and tell her the secret! But perhaps it would be better to wait. Someday, she knew not when or how, God would answer her prayers for the child. Perhaps she could satisfy her deep longing by caring for the tiny one in the basket.

"Thank you," said Dookie, "for being a good play mother." Then as the mission lady and the girl left the laundry room, the drum called the children back to school. There in the yard stood Big Mo, looking at the group of boys and girls.

"Here I am," called Dookie.

A proud smile shone on the man's face when he saw his daughter. A happy smile formed on Dookie's face as she waved back. He had been near the school all the time. Sookie was asleep, and Resa was taking good care of her. It was a happy world after all, Dookie decided as she took her place at the table to learn to make magic figures that talked.

That evening after supper, Mo and Dookie sat on the step of the home to watch the moon come up. Dookie was holding Sookie and telling her all about school. Mo listened with deep interest to the smallest detail.

"Then we had stories and songs with our fingers," continued Dookie. "When I learn to do them better, I will sing them to you, little Sookie.

"Then we went to Neda's class. She is a good storyteller, too. We took our magic sticks and made marks that are messages. Some marks say 'Jesus loves Dookie.' And when you make them backwards they say, 'Dookie loves Jesus.'"

Little Sookie did not make any comment, but she looked up into Dookie's face as though she were trying to understand.

"Now, Big Mo," said Dookie, "tell us what you did today."

Mo leaned back against the side of the door.

"I have the most wonderful work in the world," he began. "With these strong hands I help people who are in need. While you were in school I did many things for the kind doctor."

"Tell us what you did," begged Dookie.

"The doctor sent me with Tim and Orlo to bring a man to the hospital who had a broken hip. He was a big man and the boys needed me to help lift him. Then there was a woman who was burned. We brought her to the hospital to be treated."

"Were her burns bad?" asked Dookie.

"Quite bad; but the doctor has magic for burns, too. She will soon be all right, I am sure."

"Then what did you do?"

"I went alone to bring in an old grandmother with sore eyes. Dookie, how thankful we should be that we can see! But I, too, have magic, my little one. I will get it and show it to you."

Mo went in the house, took something from the shelf, and handed it to Dookie. It was long and round, and it had a shiny button on one side. On one end there was a round glass that sparkled in the moonlight.

"What is it?" asked Dookie, turning it around in her hand.

"It's a magic stick," said Mo. "The doctor gave it to me to use in my work at night. Push the button on the side."

Dookie pushed it, and a light filled the circle of glass.

"Oh!" said Dookie, nearly dropping the object on Sookie. "It surprised me. What is it?"

"It's a magic light," said Mo. "It will help me find my way when the moon is not shining. The doctor called it a flashlight, for it is ready to turn on whenever I need it."

"It is bright," said Dookie, pushing the little button up and down.

"But now it is time for us to put it away and go to bed," said Mo. "Morning will soon come. I will get a warm bottle of milk for Sookie. She will sleep well after this busy day."

144

"But she slept most of the time in a nice basket in the laundry room. The lady who takes care of her is a good play mother. And Big Mo, her name is Resa, just like my own mother."

"Resa?" echoed Mo.

"She is good to Sookie, even if she does have a sad face. The mission lady said she would not be a cross mother, so I think Sookie is safe."

"Of course," said Mo. Then he mused, "I wonder what became of the other one."

"The other what?" asked Dookie.

"The other Resa. If I could know where she went, I would like to talk to her about the God in heaven who loves all of His children."

"Do you mean the Resa that was my mother?"

"Yes," said Mo. "You see, the charm doctor had her so under his evil power that she was confused. Perhaps she would be even more afraid of me, now that I am a Christian."

"We could pray for her," said Dookie simply. "The mission lady said that God answers prayers. Sometimes He says Yes and sometimes He says No. And sometimes He says, 'Wait awhile.' But we must believe that He gives us the best answer for our needs. We will pray for my mother, wherever she is, won't we, Big Mo?"

"Of course we will, my precious."

After the simple prayer, Dookie went to her little room and lay down on her mat. Many strange thoughts about the busy day raced through her mind before she fell asleep.

Big Mo Comes Running

THE next morning at the signal beat of the drum, the children gathered in the schoolroom for the worship hour to sing songs, pray, and listen to stories about Jesus.

Dookie's eyes were wide with interest as the mission lady sang the "Jesus song." Dookie wished that Big Mo could hear her sing. Perhaps he was listening outside the door, for he was working close by. When the song ended, Dookie glanced back at the open door. The lady with the sad eyes was standing there, and she smiled at Dookie. The woman turned and disappeared. Perhaps she had heard Sookie crying and had gone to take care of her, thought Dookie.

"Listen, Dookie," whispered Luani. "Now comes the story, and all the beautiful pictures. You will like this."

Dookie watched and listened as the mission lady showed pictures and told the story of the crucifixion of Jesus. Suddenly Dookie slid off the bench and started for the door, saying, "Wait a minute. Tell them not to do it. I'll go get Big Mo!" She disappeared around the corner of the schoolhouse.

The mission lady noticed Dookie leave the room, but she continued to tell the story, and show her pictures.

Dookie ran to where she knew Mo was working. "Come quickly, Big Mo, they are getting ready to pound the nails. Come and stop them! Don't let them do it!"

Mo could see that Dookie was very much in earnest. Whatever it was must be vital, so Mo put down his work and followed the girl.

"Here is Big Mo," called Dookie, as she ran up to the mission lady. "He won't let those wicked men hurt Him."

The mission lady sensed the seriousness of the situation. The pictures and the story were so real to Dookie that she was living the experience. Big Mo was embarrassed as he stood by the picture roll and listened as the mission lady said, "I am sorry I forgot to make it clear that this story happened many years ago. These pictures were made by artists who wished to show us as nearly as they could what took place on Calvary. Dookie, it happened a long time ago; it will not happen again."

"I'm sorry, ma'am," Big Mo apologized. Then he put his arm around Dookie and walked with her to the bench. He did not scold her, for, no doubt, he would have done the same if he had been a small boy. It was all so new and real to the girl.

When school was out, Dookie went to the laundry to get Sookie, for Mo would soon come to carry the baby home. The mission lady was waiting at the door with Sookie in her arms.

"Where is the play mother?" asked Dookie.

"She went to the supply room for a few minutes. May I be the play mother until you go? I like to hold little Sookie, too, you know."

"Of course," answered Dookie.

At that moment Mo came around the corner, and soon the three were on their way home. Mo carried Sookie, and Dookie carried the small bundle.

"I will have to go back and help the doctor for a short time," said Mo, after he had put Sookie on her mat. "You are a big girl now. You can give Sookie her bottle while I'm gone. But promise you will stay in the house. Do not go outside until I return."

"Of course, I promise," said Dookie. "I always do as you say."

"You are a good girl, my precious one," said Big Mo, placing a tender kiss on the girl's forehead. "I will not be gone long."

Dookie watched Mo run toward the mission.

Then she sat on her little mat, holding Sookie on her lap. It was lunchtime for Sookie, and the milk seemed to disappear quickly.

"Shall I sing a new song, little Sookie? I don't know all of the words, but someday I will learn what the magic writing tells me. Did you know that the magic writing can sing, too?"

Sookie did not answer, of course, for she was busy with her bottle; but her eyes twinkled as Dookie sang. Suddenly Dookie stopped singing. She saw something big, black, and ugly on the floor. It was crawling toward the mat. For a moment Dookie was frightened, not knowing what to do. The big stick was in the corner by the door, and the crawling thing was between her and the stick. Dookie curled her bare feet under her, and covered them with a blanket that had been folded up on the mat. Again she looked at the black thing on the floor and whispered, "A scorpion!" She had heard that the sting of a scorpion is very painful, and it might be worse than some snake bites! She covered Sookie up, bottle and all, and waited for Big Mo to return.

Suddenly she remembered what the mission lady had told them at school. "Whenever you are in danger, pray, and God in heaven will send His angels to keep you from harm."

Dookie closed her eyes and prayed. When she looked again, the scorpion was not crawling; it was standing still in the middle of the floor.

"I wish Big Mo would come home. He would

know what to do!" Dookie waited and waited. Sookie had gone to sleep under the blanket, but instead of putting her on her own little pad, Dookie held her close in her arms. The girl sat very still, scarcely breathing for fear the ugly creature would start crawling again. It was getting dark in the room, but she could still see that object on the floor. If she had Big Mo's magic light, she could be sure that it would not crawl upon the mat; but Mo had taken it with him.

Sookie pushed away the warm blanket. Dookie tucked it more firmly around the baby's feet. She looked again. This time the scorpion was crawling toward the doorway of her room. She prayed again, and thanked God for making the scorpion go away. Then she heard Big Mo singing as he came toward the house.

"Be careful, Big Mo," called Dookie. "There's a black scorpion in my room."

Mo opened the door and turned his flashlight in Dookie's room. He saw the unwelcome visitor and quickly destroyed it with the stick beside the door. Then he gathered up his two girls and held them close.

"I did not intend to stay so long," he said, "but the work took more time than I expected."

"What happened?" Dookie wanted to know.

"A man was clawed by a bear, and the doctor wanted me to help him sew the torn flesh."

"Oh," said Dookie. "You can do so many good things, Big Mo."

150

The Night Prowlers

SEVERAL months passed, and each day brought changes. The hot, dry season had gone and the big rains came. Dookie was no longer afraid when the thunder boomed and rolled across the sky. She knew that God was not angry, but He was sending the rain to make the rice grow so the people could have food. But baby Sookie cried when it thundered, for she was too young to understand. At such times Dookie rocked the baby in her arms and sang the songs she had learned in school.

It was fun to play with Sookie, for now she could sit up alone on her mat. When she played with her brown toes, she would laugh. Big Mo or Dookie would peek around the corner of the doorway and squeal at her.

"When will she walk?" asked Dookie one evening as she and Big Mo were playing with the baby on the floor.

"In another month she should take a few steps," said Mo. "As soon as her little legs are strong enough to hold her weight."

"I want her to play 'Get me' like we did when I was little," said Dookie.

"I think it is time for Sookie to be in bed," said Mo. "How about showing me some more magic figures, little teacher?"

After Mo had put Sookie to bed, he lighted the oil lamp on the bench. Dookie was eager to show what she had learned, and, without realizing it, she was teaching Big Mo to read and write. How she laughed when he made a mistake! "No, no, Big Mo," she would say. "You make the hooks on the figures too big. I guess it is because your hands are so big. But I love you just the way you are!" And then Dookie gave him a big hug.

"Now it is my turn to write some magic figures that will tell you something," said Big Mo. Very carefully he formed the characters that said, "It is time for Dookie to go to sleep. Good night, little teacher."

Dookie wrote on the other side of the paper, "As you say. Good night, my Big Mo." Without another word, she put away her magic stick and went to her room.

Mo went outside to check on Spindlelegs and Frisky. He thought of his two little girls in the room. How he loved them! They had filled his life with happiness. Sookie means joy, while Dookie means grief. Mo had thought that perhaps he should change Dookie's name to Suryakantham, which means "sunbeam," but somehow Suryakantham did not seem to suit her. She would still be Dookie to him.

Big Mo was tired, for it had been a long day of work. But before he stretched out on his mat to sleep, he knelt, folded his hands, and bowed his head. He thanked the kind Father for His many blessings: for his home and children, for the opportunity to work for the good doctor at the mission hospital, and for the school Dookie attended. Then he asked for protection during the night, that no harm should come to his little girls. Mo said Amen, and in perfect trust lay down on his mat to sleep.

From the adjoining room he heard a faint sob. Then a voice said, "Big Mo, this time you forgot to kiss me!"

Mo had not intended to hurt Dookie; he had really forgotten. Quickly he went to the child's bed and, bending low, placed a tender kiss on her forehead. "Thank you, Big Mo," she said. "Now I can go to sleep."

Mo was soon asleep. How long he slept, he did not know; but he was awakened by a wild scream of terror outside the door. The scream was followed by the snarling and barking of savage jungle dogs. From the path that led to the mis-

Reaching for his flashlight, Mo went to the door. He could see two men running. Behind them, snapping at their heels, were jungle dogs.

sion he heard another scream. Reaching for his flashlight, Mo went to the door. He could make out the figures of two men running, and behind them, snapping at their heels, were jungle dogs. How many there were, Mo could not make out in the circle of light as he flashed it in their direction. In a moment they were gone, and all was quiet.

"Who were they?" Mo wondered. "What could they want here at this time of night?"

He looked at the girls and found them sound asleep. The strange noise had not awakened them. Mo lay down again and closed his eyes, wondering who the unknown visitors could be. "Perhaps I will know in the morning," he said to himself.

Little Mali

WHEN morning came, Mo and Dookie took baby Sookie to the mission as usual. The doctor sent Mo to help Tim and Orlo and some of the older boys clear the ground west of the hospital. Roots and stumps that had been upturned when the ground was plowed had to be piled up to dry for firewood. Soon the fertile ground could be planted to beans or other crops.

"Did you hear the news?" asked Tim as Mo came to help him with a heavy stump.

"No," said Mo, wondering what it could be.

"Didn't you hear the commotion last night?" asked Orlo. "It seemed to come from over your way."

"I did hear some jungle dogs barking," said Mo; "but I couldn't see who they were chasing."

"Two men were found badly clawed and scratched not far from the river road," explained Tim. "They had been drinking, and were taken in for disorderly conduct. One of them was a charm doctor from the Savara village to the south."

"Yes," added Orlo. "They were released from jail only a few weeks ago. Now they are back again. When will some people learn to leave rice whisky alone?"

As Mo worked, he listened to the comments of the boys. It was a strange coincidence: the charm doctor, and probably Sookie's father, and jungle dogs. Mo wondered why the charm doctor had come so near to his house. Was he intending to bring harm to Dookie or baby Sookie? Why had the little one's father come so far north, if not for some evil purpose?

Surely the Lord had sent His angels to guard the home, so that no harm had come to the little girls.

"Will you help us, Big Mo?" called Addu, who was working with Con, trying to pull a gnarled root from the ground. Mo hurried over, and in a short time the root was added to the pile.

Near this plot of plowed ground were several small gullies and washouts, where streams had flowed during the heavy rains. Across one of these streams was a crude bridge used by the people who lived in the wooded section of the three hills. As Mo was carrying a bundle of roots

157

to place on the pile, he heard someone calling. He looked up to see a woman standing on the bridge. Evidently she had been crying. Mo walked toward her, thinking he might be able to help her. But she called to him, "Don't come any nearer." Thinking it was because she was afraid of Christians, he said, "I will not hurt you. I will help you if you will let me."

"I am sick," she said. "My husband is sick with the fever. The charm doctor came last night, but he did not help us. My little boy, Mali, is gone, and I cannot find him. I have called and called, but he does not come."

An empty feeling struck Mo as he thought of the disturbance in the night. Could it be that the charm doctor had stolen the boy? Surely the lad would have been found unless the jungle dogs had—but Mo did not like to think what might have happened.

"Please let me help you," said Mo. "Let me take your husband to the mission where the doctor can help. He has wonderful magic for fever and snake bites."

The woman was desperate. In spite of her fear of Christians and the curses of the charm doctor, she consented to let Mo, Tim, and Orlo follow her to her home. Addu and Con offered to search the gullies and ravines for Mali.

"He is so small," she wailed, "and he is not well. I am sure he is hungry."

When they came to the house, the boys made

a litter from tree branches on which to carry the patient. The mother searched the house again for her boy, calling in vain, "Mali, Mali, come to mother, my little garden boy." Then she fell sobbing upon the ground in a faint.

"She can't walk to the hospital," said Orlo, as he picked up one end of the litter while Tim took the other.

"I'll carry her," said Mo. "We must hurry. I will follow you." Taking the unconscious woman in his strong arms, he made his way up the path behind Tim and Orlo.

Addu and Con went along the gullies, searching for the two-year-old boy. Down over crags and tangled brush they climbed. They looked into every hold and tangled mass of debris along the banks of the washouts. They called and called, but only the echoes of their voices came back to them.

"Mali, Mali!" called Con. He thought he heard an answer to his call. "Did you hear something?" he asked his companion.

"I thought I did," replied Addu, "but it might be the myna birds calling to each other. There are so many noises in the jungle. Call again."

"Mali! Mali!" called Con. They listened anxiously, but only the echoes replied.

Addu began, "Remember the old parrot we had at the mission, and how he would mock people who laughed and children who cried?"

"Yes," laughed Con. "He even made a noise

159

like the squeak of the pulley on the well. We would run out to see who was drawing up water, and there was nobody!"

"People in the village said it was the spirits drawing water, but we knew it was only the parrot."

"There is that sound again! Did you hear it, Addu?"

"Yes, it sounded like a child crying—calling his mother. It seems to come from across the stream. We must be careful, Con, for a leopard can make a noise that sounds like a child crying. Anyway, I have my wood hatchet."

"And I have my knife," said Con. "I'm not afraid. Let's cross the stream."

Down into the water they waded, while in the trees overhead monkeys chattered and birds screamed.

"Mali! Mali!" the boys called again and again, but there was no answer.

"We must have been mistaken," said Addu. "Shall we go back?"

"We might as well," said Con.

They were about to turn back, when they heard it again—a pitiful voice calling, "Mamma, mamma! Rice, rice!"

"That was a child!" said Con, turning toward the sound.

Down in a hole filled with twigs and bits of grass they found the boy, scarcely more than a baby, thin, naked, and very dirty.

Addu picked him up and spoke comforting words to him.

"Mamma. Rice," the little one said, holding out his hands.

"We'll take you to mamma and give you lots of rice; but, first, let's give you a bath in the stream. It is muddy, but it might do some good. When we get you to the hospital we will give you a nice bath with soap. How does that sound to you?"

"Mamma. Rice," Mali said in a pleading tone.

"Mamma and rice—lots of rice," Addu promised as he bathed the child in the stream.

"You're a cute little fellow when you are clean," said Con.

But Mali was not impressed with the compliment. He only held out his dripping hands and wailed, "Mamma, rice!"

Addu carried Mali tenderly as he followed Con down the jungle path, past the crude huts of the villagers, and across the bridge and over the rough, plowed fields.

"Con," said Addu, "this little one seems hot. Do you suppose he has the fever, too?"

"It could be," agreed Con. "Do you want me to carry him the rest of the way?"

"Thanks, but I think he's asleep. I can carry him the rest of the way."

In a short time Addu placed the sleeping child in the arms of the mission lady. Tenderly she put him on a bed and called the doctor.

"They found the little boy," she said. "Shall I go and inform the mother that he is safe?"

Wiping the perspiration from his face and neck, the doctor shook his head sadly. "There is no need," he said. "The father was dead on arrival and the mother—I did everything possible, but the fever had gone too far. But come, let's look at the child. Perhaps there is still hope for the little orphan."

"The poor little fellow is half-starved. There is no way of telling how long it has been since he has eaten a bowl of good rice. No doubt he has existed on whatever he could find."

The doctor examined the sleeping child. "I will do what I can," he said. One of the nurses, Su Maree, was given charge of Mali. She gave him a bath and carried out the doctor's instructions.

Dookie's Big Surprise

WHEN school was out in the afternoon, Dookie went over to the laundry to wait for Big Mo. In her hands she carried some papers. She knew he would be proud of them, for she had worked carefully on them. Neda had given her a little star to stick on one of them because it was the best Dookie had ever done.

Resa was holding Sookie when Dookie entered the laundry. The mission lady was talking to Resa in low tones. She paused to say, "Dookie, the doctor wants to see Big Mo as soon as he comes. How would you like to stay here and visit with Resa? I am sure she would like to see your papers. She is interested in the things you do, and you can spend the time singing some of your new songs and getting acquainted with Sookie's play mother."

"I would like that very much," said Dookie shyly, as she looked up into Resa's face. There was a pleasant smile on the lips of the Indian nurse as she held out her hand to Dookie and drew her close.

"We will have a wonderful visit," she said as the mission lady left to find Mo.

The man was coming up the walk, so the mission lady called to him and together they went to the hospital to see the doctor. Mo made inquiries about the lost boy, and he was glad to learn that the little fellow had been found.

"Would you like to see him?" she asked. When Mo nodded, they went to the room.

"He's just a baby!" said Mo, as he stood by the bed. "And he is so thin."

"Yes," she said. "It is pitiful. So many of the people in the hills are brought to us in this condition. Often it is too late for us to do anything for them, as it was for this child's parents."

Mali stirred, whimpered, and then opened his eyes. He looked around and then up at Mo. He held up his thin little arms and said, "Mamma. Rice."

Mo looked questioningly at the mission lady. "Could I hold him for a minute? He thinks I am his mother."

"It might be a good idea," she said. "I doubt if he will have many hours in which to receive love and tenderness such as you can give him."

Then she explained to Mo about his condition.

The doctor had given him magic water in the veins. But there was so much wrong with him, and the medicines must be given with caution. One medicine might work against another to cause more difficulty, and the reaction might be fatal.

Mo could not quite understand. He took it for granted that the doctor had magic needles for all diseases. Then he remembered that it was only the God in heaven who could give life and healing.

"Hold him close to your heart while I pray," said the mission lady.

After the prayer, Mo held the hot little body close to him. The child was so quiet. Mo placed him on the bed, limp and still. His eyes were closed.

"He isn't dead, is he?" whispered Mo.

"No, but he is very weak. It is doubtful if he will live through the night. We will trust God to do what is best, for we have done all we can."

The doctor came in to talk to Mo. "Would you be willing to help me try to save the life of this child?"

"Me?" asked Mo. "I would not know what to do, but I would do anything to help him."

"Thank you, my brother. He needs healthy blood in his veins. I could make a test to see if the blood types match, and then I could give him some of your blood, which would give him strength. Would you be willing to try?"

"Of course," said Mo. "I will do anything you say."

After the blood typing was completed, it was found Mo's blood was the kind needed. The mission lady sterilized instruments, and again, prayer was offered. The mission lady and Su Maree helped with the transfusion. It didn't hurt as much as Mo had expected. The doctor explained to the man that there was life in the blood he was giving to the sick child.

After the transfusion was over, Mo was washing at the lavatory in the next room, when someone handed him a fresh towel. He looked up and saw one of the nurses.

"Thank you," said Mo, burying his face in the towel.

"I am the one who cares for your baby Sookie," she said, introducing herself. "You have two very sweet daughters."

"Thank you," he said again. "I think so, too. I love them with all my heart."

"You have done well. You have been a good father to them."

"Thank you," repeated Mo, still hidden behind the towel. "I have done my best. I want them to grow up to be respected. The mission school will help them, and I am grateful for it."

"I am grateful, too," said the nurse. "Grateful to you for your kindness. I have been visiting with Dookie, and she has told me many things. She said you wanted to find Resa, the child's

Ever since Dookie was first brought to the hospital, Resa had wanted
to take the girl to her heart. After six years the happy moment came.

own mother, in order that you might help her become a Christian. For six years I have kept my promise to you that I would not see the child; but now that I am a Christian, I come to ask you to release me from that promise so that I might tell her I am her mother, Resa."

Big Mo drew the towel from his face and looked into the woman's eyes. They were sad eyes, just as Dookie had said. She looked different now that she was a Christian. Her uniform, the way she wore her hair—he would never have known her.

"The same Resa?" Mo could hardly believe it.

"I have not told Dookie," she said. "But how I have wanted to take her to my heart ever since you brought her here with the snake bite. I kept my promise to you. We are both Christians now, and we no longer fear the curses of the charm doctor or the spirits."

"Come," said Mo. "What are we waiting for? Let's go and tell her right now. It will make her so happy."

The mission lady was waiting in the laundry for Resa's return. There was so much to talk about, and Dookie certainly did her share. Instead of going home for supper, they went to the dining hall where they sat at a little table—"just the four of us"—as Dookie expressed it. The girl's eyes sparkled as she looked at her mother.

Mamma and Rice

FOR several days Mali lay listless and wan on the white bed. He began to show improvement, and the doctor was thankful. "You helped more than you know," he said to Mo, as they stood by the little fellow's bed.

"It was really nothing," said Mo, modestly. "I was glad to do it."

Mali held out his arms to Mo. "Mamma. Rice," he said.

As before, Mo took him up in his arms and talked to him. When Mo started to put him down, the boy put his arms around his neck and clutched him tightly.

"He likes you. Mamma. Rice," said the doctor teasingly. "It seems we have another problem on our hands. What shall we do with him?"

169

"I really wouldn't know," said Mo, patting the little boy tenderly. "I know he has no parents and no one to love and care for him. But you see, doctor, I have a small house and—"

"A great big heart," added the doctor as he left the room.

Resa was bringing in fresh linens and she heard the end of the conversation.

"I think you need help with your family," she said. Then she also left the room.

Mo stood holding Mali in his arms. The boy would soon be well enough to leave the hospital, but where would he go? There was nobody to love and care for him. He needed two things, "mamma" and "rice." Mo had a good job, and he could supply the rice to nourish that thin body. Spindlelegs would supply the milk and Frisky would do her share as soon as she grew up. There would be plenty to eat.

Dookie could be the play mother after school, and Mali could grow to be a companion for Sookie. But Mo must have time—time to think about it and talk it over with Dookie. Would she like to have a brother? Or would she feel that he was taking her place? Then there was Resa, her mother. She would be a devoted Christian wife. He would leave it up to Dookie to decide.

The moon was slowly coming up behind the tall palm trees that grew along the river. Mo sat on the step in front of the new stone house with his family.

"Aren't you glad, Big Mo, that you made this doorstep as big as you did? Now we can sit on it and watch the moon come up—all five of us!"

Dookie was humming a song as she played "patty-pat" with Sookie. Mali sat on Mo's lap, patting his cheek and playfully pulling his ears. "I'm so happy," said Dookie. "I am so happy I could cry, but I won't. Aren't you glad, Big Mo, that you made this doorstep as big as you did? Now we can all sit on it to watch the moon come up—all *five* of us!"

Resa put her arm lovingly around Dookie, who was sitting on the step beside her.

"I am very happy, too, my precious one. Very happy. Now I can be your real mother, not just a play mother."

"My very own mother," said Dookie.

"Mamma. Rice," chimed in little Mali.

"God bless our family," added Big Mo, looking at his loved ones with affection.

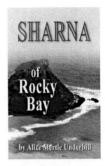

Sharna of Rocky Bay

Alice Mertie Underhill tells the story of a young girl who spent her childhood amidst the cold, rocky coves of Rocky Bay.

The Adventures of Kado

Alice Underhill's true-to-life story of a native boy and how he grows from a regular savage's child, to an influential Christian.

Other Titles from TEACH Services, Inc.

Treasure From the Haunted Pagoda

Eric B. Hare tells the way in which God prepared the 'special place' where a little boy grew to manhood among the superstitious tales of devil-worshipers.

Choma—A Boy of Central Africa

Ella Robinson's character-building story of a young African boy living in a large village. When missionaries visit the village he learns about God, the Bible.

We'd love to have you download our catalog of
titles we publish at:

www.TEACHServices.com

or write or email us your thoughts,
reactions, or criticism about this
or any other book we publish at:

TEACH Services, Inc.
254 Donovan Road
Brushton, NY 12916

info@TEACHServices.com

or you may call us at:

518/358-3494

Produced in partnership with
LNFBooks.com

CPSIA information can be obtained at www.ICGtesting.com
Printed in the USA
LVOW070259160113

315772LV00001B/44/P